Made in Africa

dwight kopp

Made in Africa Copyright © 2014

ISBN: 978-0-9895853-7-8

for my family

South-Central Africa Regional Map

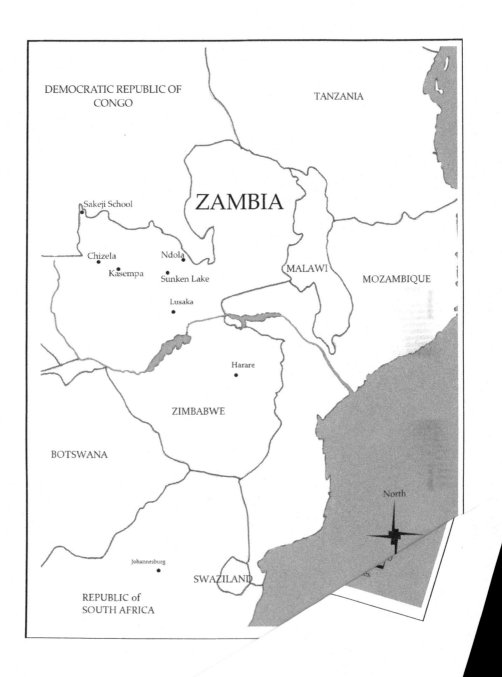

South-Central Africa Regional Map

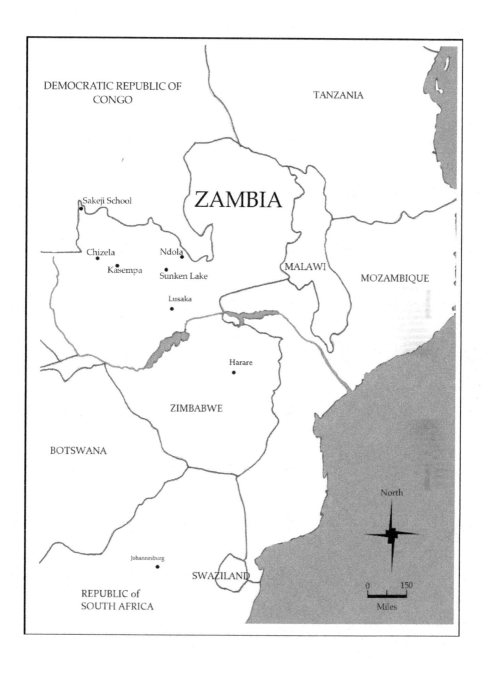

Prolog

The first day of university biology class in the States, I sat next to a black American girl. We got to talking, and she asked the dreaded question: *where are you from?*

I have no idea where I'm from.

I have a Zambian birth certificate and an American passport.

I could apply for Zambian citizenship. White Zambians *are allowed*. In fact, Zambia's vice-president is white.

Do I look at language, religion, race, or how many times I've had malaria? How does one qualify as being *from* somewhere?

Or does it matter?

People of *any* color born in America are ipso facto American citizens.

What about a white boy born in Zambia to an American born woman and an African born father? I tried to explain and ended with, "I guess that makes me African-American."

She laughed.

What does it mean to be "from" a place?

Five years later a Zambian woman asked where I was born. I told her. She laughed and said, "So you belong to the Kaonde tribe."

I laughed, too.

But it wasn't funny.

Labels get ridiculous. The black student in America may have spent her life self-identifying as an African-American without having any idea what Africa looked, smelled or tasted like. All she had was color.

I, on the other hand, have all the 'from-ness' but no color. But neither from-ness nor color can satisfy a heart's deep need for belonging.

My childhood was marked by contrasts. Compared to most in America we had next to nothing. Relative to our bush neighbors, we lived like royalty. But comparison is a poor unit of measure.

Living with a high level of disjointed, bone-jarring, cultural collision was my norm. I knew and understood both worlds simply *because* of the contrast. Contrast was all I knew. Because of it, I saw things others could not—objectively evaluating what some might take for granted. In other ways, I knew neither world, being never entirely in one or the other. I had a global world view and a deep naïveté.

Culturally, I became a nomad. Able to interact with anyone from any culture, but connecting most deeply with other nomads. Never feeling like I fit in anywhere, except with family.

Maybe that's why I want a camel.

Did you know, they can drink twenty-five gallons in less than ten minutes?

Amazing creatures.

So I inhabited the area between—what my anthropology professor called the *liminal space*. Standing apart from culture, I became an observer. Participating occasionally, moving easily from one to the other but connected to neither. A white boy, born among the Kaonde people, to an American mom and a dad who himself—being born in

2

Zimbabwe and raised in Zambia among the same people—was just as confused as I. Passports merely give access to a 'port.' They might explain the parts, but they don't convey the sum. Birth certificates, the same.

In the end, it's just paper.

As a white-boy in sub-Saharan Africa, I had to reconcile the inordinately disjointed segments on a daily basis.

I was a child on the moon.

1

Mukinge Mission Station

1974

I took my first breath at **Mukinge** (Moo-King-Gee), in Zambia's Northwestern Province. That won't mean much, unless you've been there.

But place is important, so I'll bring you up to speed. Mukinge is a bush hospital.

Bush is the African word synonymous with Australia's 'outback.' Bush isn't necessarily defined by a certain kind of climate, woodland, or the like. 'Bush' mainly refers to any location beyond the normal reach of a country's infrastructure. This is not to be confused with living 'off-grid,' or an hour's drive from a grocery store.

We lived in an area of bush characterized as the Central Zambezian Miombo woodlands. Here, most trees lose their leaves just before rainy season. The taller canopy overhung a floor of shrub and grasslands, prone to bush fires in the dry season. The grassy wetlands called Dambos, surrounding the river areas, offered wild pasturelands that supported village cattle or herds of wildlife. Hippo, sable, impala, giraffe, cape buffalo, warthog, bush pig and hartebeest gathered with zebra and lion at watering places.

Elephants, singly or in groups, roamed Zambia's wild places. Here, I've come upon elephant herds over seventy strong, talking quietly among themselves; the low, burbling, guttural noise of their conversation rolling around like music.

The infrastructure of Zambia has since expanded to embrace those farther out, but back in 1974, Mukinge was officially in the bush.

Bush hospitals survive in the most unlikely places. The woods around Mukinge stretched on forever. In the early days, Dr. Bob Wenninger, who delivered me, went hunting to provide extra food for the patients and staff. Mukinge was about as far away from a Walmart-world as one could get. At that time, power was provided by a station generator, giving three hours of electricity a day. Phone connection to the outside didn't exist. Cell and satellite phones didn't either.

Everything in the bush was more work. Kerosene for lamps had to be brought in from town. Water was pumped from the river, stored and purified. Basic food stuffs were transported from town or raised in the back yard. Bread had to be baked. Most everyone kept chickens: the one-meal-meat-creature who self-preserves until butcher time. Laundry, hot water, cooking, cleaning—all happened without external power. In an age before disposable diapers reached African markets, one can appreciate the finesse required to live in such a place, let alone run a functioning hospital.

Malaria, tuberculosis, and (early on) leprosy were common visitors in the wards.

Then there was me: a mewling, white, man-child.

Born in the middle of nowhere.

Mom and Dad worked four hours from Mukinge, at the Chizela Bible Institute—located in a more remote corner of the Northwestern Province. Dad taught Bible classes in kiKaonde, the local tribal language, and Mom, a nurse, manned the station's clinic. In the absence of a doctor, she frequently had to deal with medical crises beyond her 'pay grade' and communicated with Mukinge's doctors via radio to diagnose complicated and life-threatening cases.

For my birth, they traveled from Chizela to Mukinge—one hundred miles and four, bumpy hours. In order to arrive in time, they left two weeks before my due date. But the rainy-season excursion over pot-holed roads worked like Pitocin, and I came the next day.

I don't know what occurs when someone is born. I don't know if it was my first gulp of air or the blast of near-tropical sunshine through over-washed curtains. But something happens when a fellow is born in Africa. I've never been able to see it, but I think there might be a tattoo on my bottom that reads, "Made in Africa."

Black Zambian babies are beautiful creatures with soft curls. I was ugly, pink and wrinkled. Quite the novelty.

According to legend, Mom took an extended stay at the hospital after my birth to suffer from hepatitis A. The other missionaries took turns bringing her meals. As it turned out, the isolation ward looked out on the mortuary. Mom got to stay for a month, listening to the wailing of mourners and missing her family.

The sound of women wailing is enough to give a sober-minded priest the willies. The wailing seeps out of a bleak despair, the hollow ache transmuted into a death song. The shrill rising and falling is eerie, uncanny, and unreserved.

And Mom listened to it every day. "Woe mamma, yo yo yo. Woe is me, my child is dead." She was still learning the language but made out a few lines, "My mother hasn't heard. My father hasn't heard," as they carried a body off to the village for burial.

Under the ripening quality of Zambia's sub-tropical sun, and without the luxury of refrigeration, the dead are mourned and buried quickly.

In America, when someone dies, the family does their best to 'hold it together.' They put the deceased in an expensive box and let everyone walk past a body that's been doctored to look like it's sleeping. Then they proceed to bury that expensive box in the ground. I don't quite understand all that. In Zambia, death is louder, faster and cheaper.

To make matters worse, a case of malaria horned in on the hepatitis, and Mom was quite sick.

She mentions it like it was nothing, but I know better.

There was no parade of parents and siblings visiting Mom or the baby. My grandparents were thousands of miles away at a time when people used telegrams for urgent news.

With Mom in the isolation ward, Dr. Bob and Carol Wenninger were my first set of surrogate caretakers. They called me 'Squirt' for reasons I won't get into because this is my story, and I'll say what I like.

My parents named me Dwight.

That 'dw' consonant blend happened to fall on poor soil in a land where consonant blends are more common than fire ants. I mean, with words like Nshima, Nzango and mbututu, the consonant blend-thing should be a cake-walk. But the Zambian mouth didn't take to the word and I spent most of my life as "D. Whitey."

As if I didn't know.

Mom grew up in West Seattle. Her father—a decorated World War II veteran—returned from the war to serve time as a school teacher and later as principal. Her mother raised seven children and buried one. Mom and her siblings learned to swim in the waters off Alki Beach where the cold killed you if you didn't drown. The sky scrapers of Seattle stood across the Puget Sound and Mount Rainier hung from the sky behind them. Mom grew up on the hill, in the green house with the porch swing. They gardened out back and her mother, also an RN, cooked and canned and put puzzles together.

How many women want to leave all that, and make a permanent move to the back side of the globe to have her babies?

Mom stayed at the hospital and turned yellow. Because it was midterm, Dad had to return to Chizela without her to teach classes and burn toast. He was pretty good at toast burning, but maybe that was because Julie, my two-year-old sister was helping.

7

Somewhere in there, my mom's identical twin sister showed up in Zambia. Now I had two mothers. One white, one yellow. Aunt Cathy happened to move to Africa just in time to help care for me while mom was in the hospital.

Years later, I still ran up to Aunt Cathy, wrapped my arms around her legs and looked up into her face before realizing something wasn't quite right.

They looked alike, but were different.

2

Chizela Mission Station

1976

Perhaps a few of the Kaonde from Zambia's Northwestern Province people saw Mushala as a freedom fighter. Mushala's career began as an anti-colonial activist, but he got slighted by his own when the national government took over from the Brits. In retaliation, Mushala started a terrorist separatist movement early in '76 to rectify, he said, the neglect of the Kaonde people. He billed himself as a black Robin Hood for a province, that by nature of distance from the capital, was considered back woods.

Others saw him for what he was: abductor of women, creator of child soldiers and major pain-in-the-ass, to coin a Kaonde term.

Village lore said he could rub a leopard skin that hung from his belt and disappear. The terrorist's sorcery kept him out of sight, vanishing into thin air just ahead of Zambia's military trackers, his legend growing ever stronger. Robin Hood meets Houdini.

In an animistic culture, the division between natural and supernatural runs dangerously thin. Mushala's supernatural abilities were generally accepted as fact. Consequently, the man's wizardry was spooky enough to make seasoned soldiers trigger happy and slippery enough to exasperate the military leaders who needed to book him, bag him or beat him. Any would suffice. But it's difficult to catch someone who turns into a whirl-wind and transforms his enemies' bullets into water.

Eventually one of Mushala's wives ratted him out, exposing, like Samson's Delilah, the villain's secret strength. Apparently, said she, the only way to kill the man was to strip naked before going into battle against him. Only then might Mushala be rendered vulnerable to conventional warfare.

I suppose the sober-minded saw these legends as the rot concocted to cover incompetent military campaigns at most or poor marksmanship at least, but not me.

I believed all of it. I was two years old.

The conflict in the Northwestern Province grew and Zambia's military suffered between the scourge of the president's impatience in Lusaka and the tsetse flies biting them in the bush. Time ran out, tempers ran short and scapegoats were needed.

For my parents, teaching at a remote Bible school and tending a rural clinic, the unruly Mushala turned one of Zambia's forgotten places into a crucible.

Government trucks with olive canvas covers descended on the mission station, disgorging black men in green, brandishing even blacker weapons to stand in the shade under trees.

Whether or not these men were prepared to run naked into battle I could not say. Mostly, I remember my parent's stress at finding themselves at odds with an adolescent military force in a place few people knew existed. The soldiers blamed Dad for supplying Mushala's men with drugs. Maybe it was true. Missionaries are notorious for handing out life-saving medicines to people without requesting summaries of political affiliations. Those who qualified for medicines had fevers or tested positive for malaria.

Complicated stuff: if you're dying, they'd help you.

I was two when I burst through the screen door, exploding out of the house with a grand disregard for the state of the union, only to find the fields of slashed grass full of soldiers staring at me.

The year was 1976. My earliest memory.

I *was* a bit of an eyesore. After all, right then, I was probably one of the only white boys in a hundred miles.

Being two years old isn't easy, but it is straightforward. Two-year-olds hear and understand everything, but can't communicate. I was probably a bi-lingual listener-in and over-curious with way too much uninhibited-happy-energy for parents who hadn't expected to come under scrutiny as accomplices to an enemy of state.

I have vague recollections of whispered conversations about mission records, but maybe my mind made that up. Still, this is my story, so I can say what I like.

The soldiers found one of Mushala's men, beat a confession out of him and dragged him to our front door so he could finger the guilty medicine-giver. Mom asked me later, "Do you remember the man wrapped in a rope the soldiers had beaten? The man who claimed Dad gave him medicine? Do you remember us being escorted at gunpoint to the clinic to search for the incriminating pill bottle?"

In truth, being two years old is rather like staring at the world through a key hole. Two-year-olds don't realize that what they see is only a tiny slice of real life. Until they walk through a screen door. Like I did.

There I was, in our personal war zone, blazing white. All the juju in Africa wouldn't have rendered me invisible. If someone wanted to start shooting, I was a dead ringer. They wouldn't even have to get naked before they got started.

Just as well.

3

August 1976

Tension was thick. That's the other stuff children get. Tension. No one has to tell them.

The government's suspicion hanging over Dad and Mom extended to the nearby villagers who were considered guilty by association.

One of Mushala's wives, Rejoice, was a lovely Christian woman. She and her extended family suffered deeply under the reproach that came against them because of her husband's activity.

Fear mounted that the Chizela students might be targeted by the terrorist. Mushala already had a record for raiding villages and conscripting men and women.

Sam Kasonso, the church bishop overseeing the school, decided to evacuate the Chizela campus. Faculty, students and staff were relocated to Mukinge.

The women and children left in the first vehicles out. Lorries from Mukinge went back to move everything. Library. Chickens. Tools. Generator. Furniture. Farm equipment. Seven **lorry** loads.

Dad and Richard Soko were the last to leave. Chizela had been gutted. This was where dad lived from 1948 to 1962. He was leaving the place of his earliest memories.

No one knew if we'd ever go back.

So we moved.

We were still in Kaonde tribal land, but the sometimes-invisible bad guy practiced his rebel-magic further away.

I guess life wasn't as exciting after the move, because I only remember playing in the sandbox with another milky-white boy.

After machine guns, ropes and leopard skins, sandboxes are a bit dull.

Although Mukinge offered six hours of electricity a day instead of three, Chizela always felt more like home. Not sure why. Maybe because that was where Dad seemed most at home. Or maybe that was where he felt closest to his own father. I don't know. The Chizela bush had a deep, unhurried serenity. It was the kind of place where one could take a deep breath and feel the full effect.

Dad loved interacting with the **BaKaonde** (Kaonde people). While both Dad and Mom learned kiKaonde (the language of the BaKaonde), it wasn't exactly a calculated career move. After all, with that on a resume, a person can go places in the world. But they believed the best way to speak to a person's heart was in their own language. Over and over again, I saw faces light up when Dad and Mom used **kiKaonde**.

The BaKaonde, like many tribes in Zambia, greet by sliding their hands across each other's. This is followed by a hand-clapping that starts loud and gets softer. The longer the series of claps, the greater the honor afforded to a person. Greeting Chief Chizela required quite a series of claps starting loud and ending with hands barely patted together.

Women and men clapped differently. The women cup their hands while the men held theirs flat. The verbal greeting includes a veritable Q&A session that might go on for a while. A Zambian proverb states that a greeting doesn't cost one ngwee (penny). The "are you well?" is followed with the reply, "I have woken up."

The implication is that life is so tenuous and precious, that the mere fact of waking up in the morning is worth celebrating. And it is celebrated in the ritual of greeting every day. There is something rooted in that, I think. People who are familiar with death don't take life for granted.

Although there are over seventy different languages in Zambia, most tribal greetings follow a similar pattern.

Question: How did you wake up?

Answer: I woke up well.

If not, the greetings included a summary of symptoms including diarrhea, fever, chills, vomiting.

Then the greeting progressed to cover the related health of family and chickens and so on.

The soothing call and response was like a song people sing to each other. Like most Zambian kids, I was toted around on my mother's back, happily wrapped in a length of brightly colored **kisapi** (cloth). My earliest memories echo with the sound of kiKaonde, the gentle clapping, the real-face interaction between people and the odd congruence of my white parents in the middle of it all.

4

1978

Julie, my six-year-old sister tapped for attention. A goat-skinned drum in the living room served as her podium. She could preach a pretty good sermon from there. I managed the audience portion single-handedly.

She had her preaching notes spread out just like Dad would and somehow managed to keep her stash of pencils from rolling off the bongo. It was play, but it was serious.

Julie's text had something to do with the fact that I, the token sinner, needed Jesus. Jesus paid for my sins on the cross, so I could be forgiven and brought back into a relationship with God. Jesus ended the alienation that kept the unholy from the Holy.

It wasn't the first time I'd heard this. But it was *my* time.

Julie asked if anyone in the audience wanted to accept this gift of forgiveness.

The whole audience responded.

I was four. I went forward and marked my name down on the line. Right there by the goat-skinned drum I reached out for that gift, taking for myself a holiness I could never earn.

Even four-year-olds can make decisions that change the course of a life.

5

Ndola

1978-1979

At the request of Bishop Kasonso, Mom and Dad left Mukinge to work in Ndola at the Bible College of Central Africa (BCCA). Soon after, Dad met Baptist missionary Roger Kemp and discussed the possibility of various church denominations joining hands in their efforts to offer post-secondary, religious education. They didn't see much sense in every denomination trying to do the same thing in the same area with limited resources. They envisioned seeking accreditation from an international accreditation council to bring the college up to a Bachelor's level. Their brainchild birthed the Theological College of Central Africa (TCCA) out of BCCA, to create a non-denominational Bible school offering training for pastors and church workers.

In those days people wrote real letters. Imagine the complete absence of advertisements, catalogs, or junk mail. Only hand written letters with that funny smell from lick-to-stick stamps. Blue air-mail forms, folded and sealed along the sides—the paper making itself into an envelope, so it was lighter. I guess an extra two grams made all the difference. Because each letter had taken at least two weeks to get there, they had a tired look about them as if suffering from jet lag or wrinkled clothes from sitting too long.

Letters came from Julie, too. She started attending **Sakeji** (Sah-KAY-jee)Boarding School. What I didn't see through my keyhole, at age four, was the resurgence of military tension between Angola and the Democratic Republic of Congo. Sakeji nestled on a finger of Zambia thrust up between conflict zones. Armies needing to move from one to the other found it easier to cross through Zambia instead of going around. As a result, Sakeji found itself sitting uneasily on the sidelines of war. Troop movements garnered international attention. International attention doesn't mean much until your relatives in Seattle hear about armed conflict and wonder if the grandkids are okay.

That year, the rains were so bad that the dirt roads up to the school were impassable. Kids were piled into the back of straw-lined lorries (trucks) and transported to Mwinilunga over forty miles to the south where parents were waiting.

Letters also came from Grandma and Grandpa Kopp in Portland, Oregon. The Bible School at Chizela was part of Grandpa's legacy to Africa. Joseph and Mary helped start the school in 1948 at the request of Charles Foster. But now Grandpa had a brain tumor, and I imagine every letter Dad wrote them had an unwritten question at the end. Was he still alive?

Late in 1979, we traveled to the United States for six weeks. To say goodbye. I stood next to the hospital bed holding the hand of the man who first took the Kopp family to Africa. I remember the scar on his head from surgery.

And I know he prayed for me. I can't tell you how I knew that. I suppose one just feels it. A man praying for you who's that close to Heaven leaves a mark, too. The good kind.

Grandpa was a man sure of where he was going, but sad that he couldn't watch his family grow up around him. I don't remember despair. Maybe the smell of hospital coffee, flowers and disinfectant, but not fear. Grandpa had a deep kindness that still

18

makes me cry. A father-love that so few these days know anything about. That kindness is part of my inheritance.

It matters more now than it did then.

Africa had been Grandpa's idea from the beginning. In 1944, he and grandma drove from Washington State to New York City. They joined the rush of missionaries anxious to get to parts distant now that the war was over. An eager Joseph Kopp trolled the docks every day in New York until he finally secured a berth aboard a ship bound for Cape Town. But the ship only took men. Grandma had to come later. Of the six civilians on his ship, four or five were headed out to begin missionary service in places like the Belgian Congo and India. Due to mechanical issues, Grandpa's ship was delayed in Florida, where he took advantage of the warm, sunny beaches. Grandma found passage one month later and the two were reunited in Cape Town. Grandma and Grandpa moved into Nkoya tribal land in the Lozi Kingdom of Zambia's Western Province to work with the Mbunda people. (It's complicated.)

Grandpa Kopp, the evangelist, canvassed villages in the area, preaching about a love crazy enough to motivate a farm boy from Washington to travel all the way to Africa. He worked with translators like Henry Kazakula and hosted meetings in the shade of mango trees. But he wasn't only preaching. There wasn't much else to do in the bush.

Grandma was found to be pregnant with twins. As the due date approached, she was carried out on a hammock strung from a pole. (The car was, for some reason, not available.) The two-day trek to Kaoma was followed by bush plane to Lusaka, and from there on to Bulawayo, Southern Rhodesia. Bulawayo offered better medical care, more suited to the possible complications when delivering twins. Tim (Dad) and Tom joined Joseph and Mary Kopp at Luampa Mission Station for a few years before the family moved to Chizela. Later, Dave, Peter and Lois were born to round out the family. Dad lived in Zambia until he was sixteen.

In September of 1979, we returned to Zambia. Africa was waiting. After a heart-wrenching goodbye, we crossed the oceans by plane. Dad knew he wouldn't see his father again.

After arriving in Zambia, we went straight to Mukinge for Aunt Cathy's wedding. I managed to play for a while before being conscripted as chief ring bearer. I was prescribed a lengthy bath designed to remove several layers of Africa acquired in our short time back.

Dr. Jim Foulkes stood in for Grandpa Wilcox to give Aunt Cathy away. Mom and Mrs. Mundambo were matrons of honor and Dad brought the special music. Julie was the flower child.

Uncle Keith Frew preached a sermon that lasted too long for my short legs, and so the ring bearer received a special dispensation to sit on the stage. But it was Africa, and an occasion so solemn as the wedding of my other mother (as figured by African tradition, Mom's twin was also my mother) was not diminished by this minor concession to the tired legs of the white boy.

So Aunt Cathy married Ken Reimer, a Canadian race car driver she'd met in Zambia. Go figure. However it happened, real old-school romance flourished right there in post-colonial Africa. The Reimers went on to make me three cousins and call Zambia home for almost forty years.

After the wedding, Dad went back to teaching at The Theological College of Central Africa (TCCA) in Ndola and I attended Humpty Dumpty Nursery School. Dick, Jane and Spot tried to teach me how to read. During recess I chased blueskop lizards (bloukop, in Afrikaans) with boys from India and Zambia and Europe. The blueskop lizard (tree agama) can reach up to fifteen inches long and made an inviting target, blue head bobbing up and down and long-nailed toes clinging to the side of a tree.

Just outside of Ndola was a place called Monkey Fountain. Here Mom and Dad completed the initial phase of language study when they first arrived in the country. But Monkey Fountain also had a zoo. I'm not sure quite why Zambia needed a zoo. Seeing wild animals was a normal part of life. But I guess the President needed a place to keep the tigers he'd been given by the Prime Minister of India. There were a few other animals there, and the standard of care was about what one might expect for a developing country.

Mom took me for a visit. We saw the crocodiles and the presidential tigers. I stared long into the snake pit. When I looked up, all the visitors had started moving back toward the main gate. It was like the tide was rushing out.

"What's going on?" Mom asked.

"Don't run," we were told, "but the lion has escaped from his cage."

Underfed lions, perpetually prodded and teased by children, developed a certain proclivity for hunting down said little people and making them disappear.

Don't run?!

Mom took my hand, and we marched back to the vehicle, at speed.

Just another day at the zoo.

I never heard if they found the lion.

6

1979

One month after we arrived back in Zambia, Joseph Kopp crossed over.

He traveled by death, which is faster than planes, but harder.

I've never met someone who stared death down with such gentle courage.

I crawled on Mom's lap, and we cried. Julie was away at boarding school.

Dad's college students came and sat with us. Zambians know how to care for the grieving. They didn't talk or offer useless words, but sat and helped carry the grief for a while before another group took over. They knew Mom and Dad had returned to Zambia for them. And so they honored the patriarch of my family with silent comfort, making sure Dad and Mom were never alone.

More airmail came and went. There may have also been a telegram.

In truth, the only letters I remember well came from Mom and Dad. The letters we got at boarding school.

Because once you go to boarding school, no other letters matter anymore.

7

1979

Sakeji Boarding School is about as far away from anywhere as you can get, short of setting up camp in the middle of the Sahara. In truth, I'd rather have left this part out. I just look at school pictures and there it is: the tattered hole in my childhood I'd rather not talk about. I suppose everyone has one of these.

This is mine.

Home school was in its infancy and not well regarded. Socially, I was a misfit in the bush. The government-funded education available to rural children would have severely curtailed any chance of higher education. The opportunities for peer interaction with kids my age were limited. At that time, boarding school seemed like the only real option.

That's just what parents did then; it's all there was.

And it hurt like hell.

I was five years old when Mom and Dad settled us into the Cessna single engine plane and hugged us goodbye one last time. I knew it was coming. Julie had done this before. I watched her go off to school, disappearing from my life for months. It was my first time. I'd been to Sakeji to pick Julie up from school, but my folks wanted me to get a feel for Sakeji before we went back to the States for furlough. They figured it would make the transition easier after our stateside trip.

The plane taxied down the grass airstrip at Mukinge mission station and turned at the bottom end. The engine wound up and we bumped our way over the grass strip, craning our necks to get one last glimpse of Mom and Dad before the plane lifted off.

I cried. Julie cried. Mom and Dad cried, too.

Planes lie. They make you feel closer than you are. Planes skip over all the dirt roads and rain filled pot holes, the trees blur beneath you and a child can be misled into thinking his folks could pop in at any time.

A week is a long time for a five-year-old. A three month term is forever. I remember snatches of those first days. The complete bewilderment. The fear. I was being led down a long dark tunnel and couldn't do anything about it. Julie was a mess. I knew that, somehow. I know it more now. I kept asking her how long until Mom and Dad came to get us. I must have asked every time I saw her the first three weeks. Every time. Five-year-olds can't conceive of time spans longer than a few hours. Three months was the life equivalent of at least a year for an adult.

Sakeji was established as a school in 1925 for missionary children. It provided a first-through- seventh grade alternative to sending children abroad. Before Sakeji, children of missionaries or other expatriates living in Africa were left in Europe to attend school. Africa tended to be fatal for children, so they were often left behind. Some were reared entirely by aunts and uncles.

We **piccanins** were herded into the meeting room at the end of the dorm. The seventh grade boys picked "little brothers." I got two big brothers. Mark Frew and Greg Bakke agreed to split the term. Mark already had a real brother there. Ian Frew was a year older than I. The Frews had lived with us at Chizela. Greg came from Mukinge. It should have felt like old home week.

It did not.

A big brother was responsible for orientation. Helping to get life sorted. But how is a five-year-old supposed to get life sorted when his parents suddenly disappear?

It helped some to know that Dad attended the school from 1953 to 1960.

Narrow beds were arranged barracks style under mosquito nets that dangled like a mass of cobwebs beneath open-rafter ceilings. My vintage valise of personal effects perched on the chair between my bed and the one beside it.

I shivered into pajamas, endured the first night of devotions and climbed into bed with springs that squeaked on the iron frame. A mosquito net pulled down and tucked underneath. My bed became my first escape. The only place where I was able to think about Mom and Dad without interruption.

I cried myself to sleep, lonely beyond words.

8

The morning bell rang, dragging me back into the dreadful reality of another day away from home. Every day was programmed, planned and managed. I'd like to say I bounced back, jumped into the routine of school and forgot about missing my folks.

Fifty boys scrambled to make their bed, complete their devotions (with the help of their big brother), dress in clothes that were only washed every three days, pull socks up to the knees and hustle off to breakfast.

I had to wait for my big brother to tie my shoes. Fear entered my young heart.

What if I were late? But someone tied them and the troop of boys spilled out of the dormitory and across the parade ground. Some of us sat on the concrete stairs by the dining hall to wait for Miss Halls or Miss Hoyte to shake the wooden handle of the dinner bell so the hammer clattered under engraved brass. Then boys and girls, tired, numb and teary-eyed, streamed into the cafeteria, pulling checkered serviettes from numbered boxes before standing behind chairs at assigned tables. Children stood silent, waiting for the headmaster to give thanks for the food. One hundred heads bowed in unison.

In 1979, most students at Sakeji were white. A few black Zambian's added much needed color. The school represented what might have been the largest collection of white children assembled in Zambia. Their backgrounds varied.

When the Head Master finished praying, one hundred chairs scraped over concrete and we sat. During my dad's time, meals were silent and students learned to interact with hand signals which developed into a pidgin sign language.

We were allowed to talk.

But the menu hadn't changed. Feeding that number of kids in a place where grocery stores didn't exist represented quite a feat. I lived in complete oblivion to this daily miracle. Our meals at home certainly didn't represent an extraordinary variety, but there's something special about a meal your mom cooks for you.

Because of my parents' work and example, I understood how rude it was to turn my nose up at someone else's food. When you're sitting in a dark hut and someone offers you food, you eat it. In most villages, our visit precipitated the demise of a precious chicken, the equivalent of emptying a savings account. Meat didn't normally make it onto their menu. To be served meat was an honor. Hospitality like that cost them dearly. It would never do to refuse.

At Sakeji every last bit of food at every meal had to be eaten, too. This wasn't unusual for me. That was just like home. The food, however, wasn't. Most of the time, the practice of finishing everything on my plate didn't pose a problem.

Most of the time.

Serviettes, washed once a week if memory serves, were returned to brightly painted, wooden boxes, stuffed in over the number label that was me.

The once-a-week-serviette-washing wasn't a problem, save for the fact that we had liver on Thursdays. The eat-all-of-it serving arrived in an unappetizing chunk. Because every table had a teacher at the head, the method of disposing the liver turd on my plate required a calculated plan. Some children cut the offending organ into tiny morsels which were swallowed whole. I preferred a more direct, hurry-through-it approach. I cut the offal into quarters, held my breath and got busy.

27

Depending on the cut, this strategy shortened the ordeal. Other times, I hit a piece of gristle which refused to pass. Chew though I might, and despite frequent attempts to swallow, I eventually had to breathe. And with a breath, the foul smell filled my head. The lurching began deep in my stomach, a primal rebellion to what was *not* real food. Faced with the threat of vacating the unused portion of my stomach across the table, I quickly 'wiped' my mouth with the serviette, discarding the masticated mess into the fabric. If the opportunity presented itself, I shook the contents discretely onto the floor.

On at least one occasion, I had to leave chewed remains within the folds of my serviette, stuffing the whole business into my numbered box before I left.

Africa's insects are pioneers in recycling.

Exactly how they found it one can never be sure, but the following day, my serviette and its immediate neighbors became the epicenter of a veritable swarm of ants. They lay-to so thickly, the entire mess looked like a burnt out city block.

The black mass of ants kept other students from their serviettes and effectively blocked the flow of program.

Miss Hoyte, ever practical, grabbed the offending serviette, took it outside and shook the ants and bait into the dirt. For a fleeting moment, I feared discovery. But the gristly mass bore no resemblance to real food, which, of course, it was not.

I'm sure Miss Hoyte knew exactly what to make of the infestation every Friday but had long before determined not to make a mountain out of an ant hill, so to speak. I should probably write and thank her.

According to Dad, Ms. Hoyte still remembers all of us by name.

For the most part, the boarding school menu was palatable. As Mr. Ingalls said, "Hunger is the best seasoning." A daily dose of runny, full-kernel corn porridge in the morning, an evening round of locally grown pineapple, and the unfortunate inclusion of a watery rice-pudding offered no real challenge compared with the ordeal of

Thursday's liver. I grew to love the mushy fried cakes of rice (rice cakes) with Marmite. Vegemite sometimes made it into the seconds line as a concession to kids whose families hailed from Down Under.

One Sunday evening we were served tomato soup. Fine white, noodley bits floated to the top of oily broth. When the teacher at our table started removing these portions to her plate underneath, I took a closer look.

Every noodle had eyes. I followed her fine example, sharing wide, sideways glances with the kids around me. Worms.

We fished them out as best we could. At last, our table was dismissed to join a line of kids along the side of the dining hall for seconds. But as we neared the battered soup cauldron, I realized only a few kids were actually taking more.

My turn. I grabbed the ladle. A single stir of the watery broth solved the mystery. Worms swarmed up from where they had settled, turning the hot soup into a snow globe gone terribly wrong.

In spite of all this, few students ever reported late for meal time. Those who did come late had to walk through the throng of eating students and report to the headmaster. I was only late once. I have no recollection as to why.

I stepped into the hall, horrified that I missed prayer. I didn't think God would strike me dead, but I wasn't sure about the Head Master. Terrified, I crossed the dining room to report to Mr. Foster. I stood there, waiting for him to finish his mouthful, studying the freckles on his arm. I was rarely that close to the man. He wore a green plaid button down shirt and safari suit trousers. His tall grey socks submitted to their place, pulled up with folded over tops, just below his knees.

Finally the man spoke.

"Yes?"

"I'm sorry. I'm late, sir."

This was it. I was going to get it for sure. I'd never once set foot in the Headmaster's office, situated off the meeting hall. This was my chance.

Mr. Foster was a tall, lanky man. His body carried no extra weight, except when the girls, who sometimes crowded around, hung off his arms demanding rides. They laughed and giggled, blissfully unaware of the man's role as chief enforcer of discipline for the boys. (A female teacher usually paddled the girls.)

I was not blissful. And I was certainly not unaware. The Headmaster was the swinger of the paddle. I never considered skipping up to him with giggles and fluff to ask for a turn to swing from his arms.

Silly girls.

Mr. Foster stared down at me from his seat, taking a moment to wipe his mouth on the serviette before placing it back on his lap.

"You must march five times around the parade. Don't let it happen again."

I nodded, dumbly, and retreated to my seat, avoiding eye contact with the other kids.

"What happened?" They asked.

"I have to march." I whispered. Oh, the shame! I had to join the procession of students pacing off their penance one lap at a time on the marching ground in front of the dormitory.

"He must like you." They replied.

Me? Really? To be sure, marching beat the paddle, hands down. Still, to think that the headmaster actually knew anything about me, was shocking. Apart from the briefest of interactions during mail call, that was the only time I recall actually speaking to the man, or he to me.

9

In the absence of a kindergarten, all the youngest children marched in lines to Miss Ross's class. She was old enough to have been Dad's first grade teacher, which, in fact, she was.

Miss Ross got right into education. Though I don't remember a blessed thing, except feeling the loss-canyon of homesickness so huge I couldn't understand why everyone else couldn't see it. At boarding school, the answer to homesickness was 'busy.' I didn't receive a single hug the entire term. For a kid whose parents hugged him every day, I was starving.

Samuel Logan was my friend, one of those gifts from God that made the intolerable, bearable. I've never thanked Sam for that. He was snappy-eyed and energetic. Sakeji was our only point of contact. Unlike Ian Frew or Martin Kemp, I never saw him outside of school. While fear made me behave despite the festering ache of homesickness, Samuel did what he wanted.

He paid for it, too. I remember the time he reported to the Head Master's office wearing every pair of underpants he owned. His reasoning was sound. The more padding the better. But "Logeez," as we called him, didn't carry extra weight and the bulging buttocks caught Mr. Foster's attention. Logeez return on that investment wasn't so good. He ended up having to ankle the padding and take it on the bare. His pain equaled his disappointment. I never heard of anyone else trying that.

Logeez suited me. He was indomitable. Not that I knew that word then. I admired his grit and humor and pride in spite of ever-present rules and the shadow of a wooden paddle. He was grubby, wiry and strong. Somehow, he managed to keep himself intact while I retreated.

Becoming blood brothers was his idea. He bravely cut his hand open to procure the necessary ingredient. Cutting myself open seemed a bit rash, so I decided to pick the lid off one of my many scabs instead. The pact was sealed.

Once we were talking in class. Miss Ross walked by and rapped our heads with her bony knuckles, usually an effective focus recalibration.

It didn't work. We kept chatting and were summoned to the front for a hand-smack with the wooden ruler. I was mortified. Samuel bravely went first. He placed his hand in Miss Ross' upturned palm, took his lumps and returned crying to his seat.

My turn. I put my hand in her upturned palm and watched the ruler rise menacingly before it came down.

I've always been quick. My scared knuckles disappeared and the ruler landed hard on Miss Ross's palm.

Miss Ross was not impressed. She grabbed my hand again, anchoring it this time securely with her own slightly-red palm and gave me double for my efforts. I followed the trail of tears back to my seat and sat next to a sullen Logeez.

My knuckles burned, but it remained my one, small victory against colonial England.

Miss Eastbury was the dorm mum. She was singly in charge of fifty boys. She drove the fingernail scissors which cut so close they hurt. Miss Eastbury made her rotation during bath time, vigorously scrubbing ingrained dirt from our feet. The older boys relaxed in the tub with wash cloths artfully placed like the maple leaf on

Michelangelo's David. Miss Eastbury herded us through bedtime drills. Lines of boys brushing teeth at a long row of sinks.

Now, looking back, I think she must have been a large-hearted and talented woman with the patience of Job. Back then, she was just the one who drove the fingernail scissors and kept me moving.

Lunch followed morning class. Some afternoons we'd head down to the river for swimming lessons. Maybe that was the weekends. I've tried to forget most of this.

But I remember the *first* time I walked that path with all the other kids. People said I smelled bad. They weren't kidding. The school had no electricity save what was provided from the waterwheel along the Sakeji River, a tributary of the Zambezi. Light bulbs hung bare on black wire, pulsing erratically with current fluctuations. Instead of providing illumination, the lights created the aura of an off-record interrogation room.

And the bathrooms, dark and shadowy affairs, scared me to death. So I dropped the load in my pants. Not a great plan for a five year old, but I was surviving. I wasn't going near the bathrooms. The toilets were nothing more than privacy stalls with holes cut in the wood for seats. Down at the river, the loos weren't much better. There the filth was captured in five gallon buckets the older boys threw into the pit at day's end.

The problem with dropping one's load onboard meant I got to carry my own smell down to the river. The teachers didn't notice. The teacher-student ratio was such that I flew under the radar for several hours.

Julie admonished me to use the **loo**. Insisted on it. But instead, I headed for the pool.

The Sakeji pool was filled by water diverted from the Sakeji River through a sluice gate controlled channel. I admired the way one could turn a metal steering wheel at the top to raise the gate. I was fascinated by the water coursing in. But then, I've always been interested in the way things work. The school required that all children learn to swim. Students advanced through skill levels from

"no seal" (kids one breath away from drowning) up to "gold seal."
Those in the upper seals learned the basics of water rescue.

Kids who couldn't swim were in "no seal." That was me. We piled
into the water behind Miss Ross and her red swim cap. We shared
the dark water with frogs and the occasional snake. The pool ended
up being a decent place to get rid of a load.

I'd never thought about it before: poop floats. There it was,
appearing mysteriously on the water's surface around a now quite
relieved little boy. The intrepid Miss Ross waded in, swooshing it
aside as she passed.

One tree at the river stood out above all others. It wasn't the largest,
but it was the most significant. The Initial Tree might have been a
seedling when the school was founded in 1925, but it had initials
from students dating back to when Dad attended. I went there just to
feel close to him. It served as a talisman for many, a shared story.
Something to help us find a point of connection. But it was more
than that. There was a Presence around that tree. A Divine whisper
that reminded me—if I had been listening—that I was not alone.

Samuel Logan and I scrounged a razor blade from a pencil sharpener
and used it to cut our initials into the bleeding bark. Actually that
was his idea. He was clever that way. But pencil-sharpener razor
blades make a miserable tool for cutting into African hardwood and I
only ever managed an awkward 'D.' The initials next to mine
represented the survivors. Boys and girls who made it through
Sakeji at a darker time. A time when the headmaster often flew into
a rage and paddling morphed into beatings repressed by many.
Survivors from that era are still coming to grips with the abuse.

The Initial Tree proved they made it.

Eventually, I overcame my fear of the dormitory loos. But only
during the day. At night, bats and an occasional owl flew freely

through the open rafters. The concrete floor was cold and sported the odd scorpion here and there.

The thought of facing a wet bed the next morning prompted me to pull up the mosquito net and creep out of the boys' room. Four boys' rooms opened onto the hall. Each with twelve to fifteen beds, all shrouded with white mosquito nets. No doors. The African night was like black paint on the windows.

I began my journey, walking away from the headmaster's apartment toward the loos at the far end of the hall. Why the youngest kids' room was the farthest from the loo makes no sense to me now, but maybe they put us closest to the headmaster, in case of need. Not that I frequently saw him after lights-out.

The dark air chilled me. I kept walking. The closer I got to the loo, the farther I was from my bed. It was my own private kingdom, my own domain in a world of communal living. The only place where I could pull the covers tight around me, think about home and cry myself to sleep without anyone watching.

I kept walking until I was halfway past the big boys' room at the end. After that was only the storage room and then the loo. Almost there.

Tando slept in the last room. By the time he was in seventh grade, he weighed more than the headmaster, about which everyone had a good chuckle. The headmaster towered over six feet. Tando wasn't tall.

Before I made it past the last room, Tando snored. In my little-boy world, it was a lion. Scared white boys can run. I beat it back to my mosquito-net kingdom. There was no way I was going to be an easy white-meat snack for a lion.

It rained in my kingdom that night.

It fact, it rained just about every night that term.

10

Portland, Oregon

1980-81

Boarding school was interrupted by a two-year visit to America. I was six years old. Dad went to seminary for his master's degree, and I went to day school. My memories of that time don't stick together. They're more like individual pictures I pull out of an old shoebox.

Growing up in Africa meant that relationships with American relatives was relegated to the chunks of time we'd see them when we visited the States. Every four years I switched keyholes for a bit and the view changed.

Mom and Dad's work dictated the four-year cycle where we'd travel to the United States, so they could report to their supporters (donors). This cyclical disruption impacted all the expatriates I knew who were in a similar line of work. Later, this reporting period known as 'furlough' came to be known as *Home Assignment*, a painfully inaccurate term, if you ask the kids.

Trips to the United States always included tromping around to various churches where the family-from-Africa were put on display. This usually included Dad as special music, a three-minute ministry update, and a slide show accompanied by the song "People Need the Lord" that ended with the obligatory stunning picture of an African sunset.

The first year, we stayed in a house just down the street from Uncle Brian and Aunt Anne, Mom's brother and sister-in-law. Jaime Lynn was eight days old when they adopted her and she still had her belly-button string on.

Uncle Roger and Auntie Barbara Kemp came for a visit. Their kids, Judith and Martin, were roughly equivalent in age to Julie and me. They were friends from Zambia from Australia. (Australians living in Zambia.) It's complicated. Anyway, we took them up to Mount Hood to see snow as they'd never before had the pleasure.

There were other dear people floating past my life that year. People like the Simons, Mascords, Johannesons and Wootens. As a well-churched kid, these people framed an early understanding that a real community of faith has nothing to do with buildings.

I don't remember much else.

I do remember standing in a parking lot with Mom, watching a secondary eruption from Mount St. Helens, fifty miles to the northeast.

The second year, we lived right next to Grandma Kopp and Aunt Chris, Mom's youngest sister, lived with us for a while.

During those years I got my tonsils removed in a too-sterile hospital. I suffered the rigors of a kid shifted from one country to another and one educational system to another. I threw up in the school hallway. Several times.

Mom was concerned that I might be under stress.

Stress? Kids don't think about that. They just throw up, stop learning, act out, or wet their pants. It stopped raining in the kingdom because at home I could get to the loo without facing lions. America was reasonably benign that way.

That was also when dad gave us the 'sex-talk' over breakfast, using the 'a-okay' and index finger for clarification. I stared wide-eyed at my cheerios, remarking at their similarity to the female organ. I guess they wanted us to hear about it from them before we got 'educated' by our peers. So dad elaborated, bringing the index finger through the circle of his other hand. Kind of like a sermon illustration. We listened in awkward silence, nodding dumbly. Feeling his discomfort on the subject.

It was the first time he talked about sex with his kids. It was too early for me; sex wasn't on my radar. But some cultures sexualize early, requiring a preemptive parental strike.

American neighborhoods were laid out in neat squares with real sidewalks, gas powered lawn mowers and grocery stores within walking distance. It had parks with playgrounds and phones and television and lots and lots of white faces.

I had a few awkward friendships at school. Though I don't remember their names, I was an early watcher of people. I'm not sure I could have put it into words, but I started to recognize that not everyone felt safe when they went home. Even people who have never left the land of their birth still want to *feel like* they belong to someone. In that regard, the United States was a nation of orphans.

Here was a different kind of poverty. One deeper, more hurtful, more detrimental to the human soul than a house with a leaky roof. Here people grew up in families but felt increasingly alienated because of dysfunctions of various kinds. For some, 'family night' meant nothing. They danced around angry mothers or absent fathers, or worse. They were tended, but not cared for. Provided for, but not hugged. The absence of affection or interaction or tenderness made their homes a wasteland where escape into the boob tube offered the only reprieve from the empty, hungry silence. TV offered an alternate reality where The Little House on the Prairie played shadows over kids eating not-quite warm TV dinners by themselves.

Perhaps television didn't create the dysfunction but flourished because of it.

A family is designed to echo the voice of the Creator, validating by word and deed a person's value, worth and place.

Unlike many, I had parents who showed this kind of love. Hugs in the morning, hugs at night. Lap time. Story time. Prayer time. Snuggle time. Together time. Family night for real.

Because of that, I was one of the richest kids at school.

11

Chizela, Zambia

1982

Term Break

When we returned to Zambia, Dad served as interim principal for Uncle Keith Frew at Chizela Bible school.

I loved bush living.

Like my American peers, I grew up eating pizza. Ours was always home made from the crust up. Only a few times did elephant meat end up as a topping, and then the entire community got some. But that's because you can't eat an elephant by yourself.

It takes a village. Everybody knows that, right?

I knew you should stay downwind of a herd and watch out for mamas with calves. They kill you. It happened to someone we knew.

I'd stepped around countless elephant piles in the bush, could recognize the smell of it. We heard the elephants singing in the fields as we lay in bed at night.

But *eating* an elephant is another thing altogether.

I was eight years old. A government game warden had come to Chizela to deter the elephant herds from raiding local farms. In Zambia, monkeys were the most common garden pests. Kids sometimes spent their days in a shack by the fields, scaring them off with slingshots made of rubber cut from inner tubes. But elephants are problematic and tend to be more destructive than deer or rabbits.

Just saying.

After the government game warden had done the dirty work, the student body of the Bible school became the butchering party. We bumped along behind a sputtering tractor pulling a flatbed farm trailer. Several times, trees were cut down to make room for wide tires as we threaded our way through the bush. Someone had gone ahead to make sure the rest of the herd weren't still mourning their fallen comrade.

We arrived at the kill site. The elephant was dead and the rest of the herd moved off. Dry season grass was trampled down around the carcass where other elephants had stood waiting for her to get up.

Walking up the suspension bridge of her trunk, I straddled her neck and sat like a rajah oblivious to those laughing at the spectacle of white boy.

I sat for a while on the elephant's neck, feeling her course skin under my legs. Elephant eyelash and tail hair is strong and smooth. Like plastic shoe laces or black string licorice. Perfect for rolling into shiny bracelets and rings.

It wasn't the first time I had seen an animal butchered. But right then, I wasn't interested in meat. Wrinkles folded around one huge cow-like eye the color of amber.

Transfixed, I stared into the window of her soul. There, frozen in her memory was the unbroken ring of Africa's sunrise. It was beautiful.

I slid down from her head and walked over to Dad.

"Can I cut out the eye?" I asked.

41

Looking back now, it seems a bit dark. But, in truth, I just thought it was a beauty that needed to be preserved. That one eye, like a picture frame, captured the fiery magic and mystery of Africa's wild places. In my mind, I already had it mounted in acrylic and sitting on a bookshelf.

Dad told me to ask the warden.

I did. He laughed and said, "Go ahead."

Swiss army knives are made for boys.

Boys appreciate every single blade and its special purpose, even if there is never an occasion to use them. In fact, boys will spend time with those red knives, pulling out each blade and tool in turn, feeling the edge and *imagining* with it before putting it away.

I knew there was only one option for this job. Fighting my finger nail into the groove above the largest stainless steel blade, I pulled it open. Crouching next to the animal, I estimated how far out from the edge I needed to cut so I wouldn't damage my prize.

It would take some doing to get past the skin. After all, men were using axes to cut through the super-tough, inch-thick hide. I raised the knife, tightened my grip and brought it down hard.

Swiss army knives are *not* made for boys.

There are no safety features and those wimpy blades will close up on a fellow's fingers without so much as a by-your-leave. Red drops of blood oozed out from my fingers while I hopped around, trying to shake off the sting while ignoring the laughing game warden.

Swiss army knives might be okay for slicing bananas over cereal, they're just not up to elephants.

But I am my father's son. Dad made arrangements to retrieve the elephant's foot and ear. No sense letting them go to the scavengers. I was elated. The ear, Dad envisioned becoming a coffee table. The elephant foot—with a wood top—was to become a side table. I already saw Dad's coffee steaming on it while he sat on the couch reading his Bible. Now that's something one can pass along to the grandkids!

Mom wasn't so sure.

The students were busy working. Using bush axes fashioned from African hardwood, they chopped parallel lines in the thick hide like a macabre patchwork quilt. Machetes and bush knives separated the sections from the white fat underneath as the heavy grey skin gave way.

Once the skin was off, the elephant was eviscerated. Cutting through the belly flesh, a man hauled out the huge intestines, bulging with gas build up, slippery and white. He took it further into the bush to release the gas and clean out the stuff inside. Apparently, elephant intestines were a delicacy. I'm sure they're delicious, if you like that sort of thing. I don't. I suppose it's Africa's version of haggis.

In my estimation, an animal's organs do not qualify as food. I can eat tongue, but that's about the end of it.

Someone started a fire. Chunks of elephant meat were chopped from the flank and roasted on the spot. One sensible person had the foresight to bring salt, folded into a piece of paper.

Julie and I stood side by side while our fingers tiptoed around the hot meat to keep from burning. White granules of salt stuck to the juicy cube of roasted meat. Delicious.

And if you're wondering, it tastes like beef.

My parents, on the other hand, believe in organs. If you live in a family where eating everything on one's plate is non-negotiable, this can be problematic. Especially in the case of elephant liver.

It was delivered to our home later. The stinking, blood-loaf of an organ over-flowed the sink. I reached out a tentative finger and shoved it deep into a vessel. Black blood coated my finger. I stared it down, wondering how to run away for the time it took my family to eat their way through it.

43

God help me.

My parents agreed. It reeked so profoundly even they couldn't stomach it.

The liver disappeared.

A piece of trunk meat, prized for its marbled fat, showed up later, wrapped in a banana leaf. Dad held the piece in front of his face, staring through the nostril holes like a pair of binoculars. (Dad had an odd interest in anatomy. Another time he grabbed a still-warm lung from a slaughtered pig, put it to his mouth and inflated the organ. Science lab, bush style.)

Mom, ever the trooper, chunked the elephant trunk into kabob sized pieces and Dad sweated it through the meat grinder. They transformed the ground elephant trunk into meatloaf, which Julie and I affectionately called 'snot loaf.'

What's that topping on your pizza? Snot meat. Ha ha.

Hey. Don't judge. We lived in the bush. Didn't get out much. We took our entertainment where we found it.

The elephant foot was left to cure outside on account of the smell. Considering my frame of reference, it might have reeked awfully, but I didn't mind it so much. Most of the flesh inside had been cut away and Dad filled the cavity with sand and salt. Dad had a good time, painting the toenails red and getting it ready for his coffee. The piece was well on its way to becoming a family heirloom. Julie can have the quilt, I'll take the side table.

But the termites found it first.

I'm still sad about that.

The elephant ear hung drying on the side of the chicken house for quite a while. Its tattered edge showed the vagaries of wild living, including several bush piercings by means unknown. But elephant ears aren't flat, so Dad contrived a plywood press, put the ear between and parked the truck on top for a while.

No dice. So the elephant ear didn't make it inside either. What's the point of a coffee table that dumps your coffee off?

Pity. (Thank God, says my wife.)

I'm sad about that, too. It would have been one heck of an heirloom. Though now, being married, I understand most women don't get excited about animal parts for decor. Mom was wise enough to let Africa beat Dad at his own game.

So Africa ate my heirlooms, and I was left with a host of memories instead.

But memories are easier to pack than elephant parts. Considering we moved almost twenty times before I was fourteen, that's kind of a big deal.

In the bush, our water came from a nearby stream, pumped into raised water tanks when the pumps worked. Gravity carried water from the tanks to our spigots. That said, I remember walking to the river with cooking pots and buckets because the pumps were taking time off.

Hot water was heated in Rhodesian boilers. A forty-four gallon drum housed in mud-fired brick walls positioned over a wood-fueled firebox. The boiler sat a few feet away from an outside wall and the hot water supply was permanently plumbed to the house. No fire meant no hot water.

In the absence of adequate electricity, our refrigerator was a kerosene job. Not exactly sure how fire makes cold, but it does. Somehow. I remember seeing Dad splayed out on the floor trying to make sense of the fridge's under-things. He was often trouble shooting that way, solving problems and fixing things he claimed he didn't understand. "What are you looking for, Dad?" I'd ask.

"The obvious," he replied.

Our stove and oven were fueled by propane tanks trucked in from Ndola.

The grocery store was out back: Garden, chickens, mango trees, banana grove and hog pen. Depending on the time of year, we found fresh flowers.

Blossoming only near Christmas, flame lilies were the favorite. Julie and I hunted flame lilies to decorate. The flower's stem stood straight and proud above surrounding grass made green by seasonal rains. Their red petals leapt from the top like flames from Moses' burning bush. Once we spotted one just off the dirt road and argued about who should pick it.

Julie didn't want to get off Dad's bike, because she needed the porch step to get back on. I didn't want to wade into the grass. Why should *I* be the one who *always* had to pick the flower?

Stubborn boy, thought she. *Just like Balaam's ass. Pick the flower already*.

I hesitated. The grass surrounding the flower didn't *feel* right. Something held me back. Then I saw why. A snake moved, revealing a section of his scaly bulk roughly the diameter of my wrist.

We left the flower at-speed and hustled back to find Dad. But Dad wasn't one to go after a snake unless needs-must. And right then, the flame lily didn't fall firmly enough into the 'need' class to warrant a showdown with death. The snake was probably deadly (a safe assumption in Zambia), so the flower stayed. The snake survived. And we were spared.

Divine intervention happened more than we knew. But then, the same is true for those who daily face the snaking highways of Los Angeles.

Christmas happened differently in the bush. Dad's dad once decided to use a thorn tree for the celebration. Of all the trees growing in the bush, the thorn tree had the a shape most reminiscent of a pine tree. However, Christmas trees are notorious for being difficult to install on a good day. Thorn trees are something else entirely. According to legend, he managed to raise the tree but not without bloodshed. There's probably a parallel in that somewhere as a thorn tree better symbolizes the life of Christ.

There were no radio stations playing Christmas music in November, no advertising campaigns, no mall trips, no Christmas lists and no credit card debt. We didn't have Salvation Army volunteers ringing their bells. We didn't have family gatherings to attend, either. Except the family we created from those who lived around us.

In the absence of shopping options, we'd rummage through our closets to find something to wrap in last year's paper. We didn't have extended family nearby, but sometimes we got a Christmas parcel from America. Occasionally Christmas parcels arrived in March.

One Christmas, Julie and I followed a scavenger hunt trail to find a mewling, blue-eyed kitten still tangled with the rest of her litter. We thought we were in Heaven!

Julie and I decorated with chains we made from construction paper. One Christmas we invited neighbor and missionary Uncle Ernie to eat with us. He brought a gift of aged fruit cake he'd been saving months for the occasion. Uncle Ernie was a translator. KiKaonde hadn't been written down that long. Early literacy in many Zambian tribes followed the translation of the Bible into those languages. Uncle Ernie was a big man with a big job. He had assisted in translating the Old Testament into kiKaonde which was printed the year after I was born. Like Dad and Mom, Uncle Ernie was just another person who loved God and Africa enough to 'waste' his life in the middle of nowhere doing things no one else would ever hear about.

Animals abound in the bush. Seen and unseen. Consequently, Mom boiled all our water. This was transferred into well-used, orange-iron-stained plastic gallon jugs and tucked into the fridge to get cold. Bush or not, there's nothing like cold water to satisfy a thirsty moment.

Mom saved old cooking oil in a jug just like the water. Sometimes the jugs kept each other company in the fridge door.

One day Julie and I burst into the house, bolted for the fridge to grab the coldest jug. Warm water doesn't cut it.

Julie was born first, AND she is a girl, so I suppose it was only right she beat me to the fridge that day. She reached in, found the coldest jug and spun off the threaded lid. Little brother had to wait his turn.

He waited.

Julie leaned against the sink, upended the jug and poured the cold liquid down, determined to banish her thirst even if it took the whole gallon. She might have done it, too.

Except it wasn't water. Old cooking oil apparently does not quench thirst. It made the return journey much faster. Julie turned a shade of green I have never since seen in a human. She wretched and heaved oil-laden vomit from her mouth across the kitchen. She puked and coughed and cried all at the same time.

I cried, too. A good laugh can actually take one's breath away. And it went on for a while. Longer than her recuperation.

Maybe I was just socially deprived, but there was such a sweet serendipity to it all. Even now, she scowls when I bring it up.

Due to Zambia's proximity to the equator, the sun sets soon after six every night of the year. Electricity flowed from 6 p.m. to 9 p.m. Just like the early Land Rovers, the old generator required a crank start to get going. The greasy monster had its own shack near one of several groves of banana trees. It stayed there like a sleeping iron monster until Dad woke it up—its distant chugging could be heard from our house.

I sometimes took the few-minute bike ride with Dad at nine p.m. to turn it off. Julie sat on the bike rack behind Dad, keeping her feet away from the spokes. I followed on my own bike. One night, I decided to veer off the dirt foot path, take a short cut around the shadowy banana grove and beat Dad to the shack.

It was dark, as electricity wasn't wasted on exterior lighting.

I saw the shortcut ahead, braced for my sudden burst of speed and turned.

The bicycle stopped. Cold. My body lurched forward off the seat, crashing into the handlebars. For a moment the bike stayed upright, then fell sideways. An Angel of God had descended and blocked my way as effectively as a wall. Or in this case, a tree that had the habit of looking very much like a path.

Did I mention it was dark?

Like the apostle Paul, I had been thrown to the ground by the power of God, crying out with the same enthusiasm as the Visited. Dad and Julie returned. As I recall, they failed to appreciate the weight of my *visitation* and found, a twisted pleasure in my collision.

Darkness has a certain beauty. Or more precisely, it *reveals* beauty. With absolutely no light pollution, the wash of stars spangling overhead dazzled with the same brilliance that a city displays from an airplane. I've seen both. The Milky Way spilled like a river of white across the African sky like the train of a royal robe. A blazing magnificence. The idea of our planet being buried in something so much bigger was not just an abstract concept discussed in a classroom using Styrofoam planets swinging from hangers. Here the Southern Cross replaced the North Star. And the Milky Way was a for-real collection of the King's diamonds strewn across the black velvet table of heaven just for me. The stars burned with enough light and heat and glory to make a kid remember he is small and God is big.

The other wonder of limited electricity was silence. Without radio or television, alarm clocks, humidifiers, electric refrigerators, microwave ovens, or phones, the silence got deeper, more pure. We were without the sound of a single whirring electric motor and often without traffic of any kind, including plane, train, bus or siren.

Silence makes its own noise.

During the day, silence gave space for the click of grass under hot sunshine, the solitary buzz of a fly or the faraway sounds of drums and women singing in their fields. It gave space to hear Mom's clothes pins dropping into the cloth bag that held them, or the scratch of Dad's pen at his desk as he worked on his lecture notes, the echo of thunder hundreds of miles away, the intermittent song of birds, or the squawk of a chicken happy to find a grasshopper.

At night, elephants called back and forth on their way to undo the farmers' work in the peanut fields. Inside, moths crashed through the candle light to land with singed wings and a thump over the game of Rummikub® or Yahtzee® where the silence gave space for extended family time. We heard the pop and sizzle of locally grown popcorn on the stove. (Mom knew how to make the real thing.)

Instead of TV, we watched the world through the living room window. A paradise fly catcher built her nest nearby to show off her cascading tail feathers. From that window we saw clouds building at the end of dry season and watched wind blow the rain through trees.

News from outside came via short wave or inter-station radio. Three times a day Dad sat in the office, checked in with the operator and passed along whatever happened to be important.

The transmission coordinator started the broadcast:

"Good morning this is niner juliet echo three-eight-four calling eight-seven. Eight seven are you there? Over."

87: "Roger that. Over."

I loved to listen to the chirp and whistle of that radio, to watch the red needles, to see Dad lean over and close his eyes so he could hear better, straining through the static for the voice of someone on the outside, spelling out words with that nifty Alfa-Bravo-Charlie stuff.

The moderator called in all the stations across the country. I learned to listen then. To listen to how a word was said. And I listened to the silences.

If a station failed to report for two days, it was cause for concern. Someone would be dispatched to check on the situation. Occasionally, a station operator indicated a thunderstorm in their area, signed off immediately and unplugged their antenna. No sense letting the radio get cooked.

The transmission coordinator queried each station for messages.

87: "Do you have any messages? Over."

87: Yes, I have three messages for 89. Over."

If weather interfered with reception, or the distance between stations was too great, messages were passed via a relay system in a grown-up version of whisper down the lane.

But the shortwave wasn't for entertainment. The 7:30, 10:30 and 5:30 radio call-up provided an essential link to get necessary medical information, notify each other of travel plans, estimate times of arrival and planned routes. Travel in those days involved long stretches of horrible roads. Most traveled with gerry tins full of extra fuel, axes for tree removal and winches for tight spots.

A mechanical failure in the bush sometimes meant sharing space with hungry, wild things. In the bush, animals don't have fences to keep them in. There is a remarkable difference between a fenced-in lion and a free-roamer. Some towns in America have 'Duck Crossing' signs to protect the ducks. 'Beware of the lion' signs in Zambia are to protect the people. Elephants, lions, leopards and hippos did their share to keep life interesting in the bush.

The people one occasioned in the bush, however, were safe. Zambia's culture of hospitality ran deep. But vehicles don't naturally break down in convenient places.

Radio call-up saved lives and was a forum for prayer requests. Every station kept a log book, carefully documenting each transmission, cataloging the 'just coincidences.' A host of 'just coincidences' stacked up over years to credit the Author of Coincidences. Blue ink on cheap paper served as a reminder of The Presence in wild places. God—apparently—was quite comfortable there.

In the bush we had music from a cassette player wired to a transformer and a twelve volt battery. Dad also played the guitar. We'd sit around and sing together.

My favorite, though, was the sound of Zambians singing. Africa's voice, unencumbered by anything synthetic and undergirded by the goatskin drum was majestic and haunting and powerful. The simple joy and exuberance of life so foreign to a developed nation was most alive in the sound of Zambia singing. A lead might call out a single line of song and the body of singers responded in perfect time. Powerful. Immediate. Strong. Bodies moved in synchrony, dancing and clapping. The poly-rhythmic texture of the drumming contradicted the voices at times, but the complexity added momentum, strength and passion. A drummer might scamper away with his own pulse, the beat sounding like a rock tumbling and rolling down a hill before falling in perfectly with the others.

Brilliant.

If only this white boy could dance…

12

In Zambia, rainy season started when the first drops kicked up dust on the dry ground in October and continued until water filled every pothole and depression on the roads. The rain came in stormy, tropical bursts between intervals of bright sunshine. Because all the roads in the bush were dirt, the rain made an exciting obstacle course. Maybe it is just a guy thing. I dunno. Perhaps it was the absence of television, electricity or entertainment, but I relished the prospect of our vehicle getting stuck.

The sound of tires spinning in mud filled me with a happy-anxious anticipation. Wanting to get out, but not too soon. I think Dad enjoyed the challenge, and Africa excelled at dishing up interesting puzzles.

If other people were around (i.e: we were near a village), the men and boys gathered at the corners of the truck to push. I couldn't say for sure if the men enjoyed it, but the prospect of a mud and rubber challenge worked like a happy-shot for the village kids, too.

Bush roads were empty and relatively untraveled. Getting stuck in the bush required a different approach. Dad scoured the bush for branches to put down in front of the tires, giving them some purchase. Dad was a MacGyver. (For my young readers, that's a fix-anything-with-nothing kind of guy. You should watch more T.V.) After all, a man doesn't thrive in the bush if he isn't willing to make do when needs must. Like most Zambians, Dad could transform an old bicycle tire (**malekeni**) into an effective bungee cord with the best of them. To this day, he keeps malekeni in the boot (trunk) of his car. Dad probably got the can-do-with-almost-anything spirit from his father.

Early bridges were not much more than a couple of long stout tree trunks spanning a creek with lateral poles lashed on top to create a sort-of surface. This kind of bridge chatters quite a bit when one drives over it, the uneven poles get mouthy under the weight and the whole business functions like a bush version of the rumble strip. The problem with a bridge like this is it becomes a sort of supply station for anyone building a hut, the pre-cut poles being too convenient to pass up. Consequently, in the early days it was not uncommon to come upon a bridge in a state of un-dress.

As the story goes, Grandpa Kopp drove unhesitatingly out onto a bridge that ended in the middle, save for the beams spanning the river. I don't know how Grandma responded when she saw him racing toward a certain end, but he stopped short of the precipice. He got out without a word, pulled up the poles behind the car, moving them to the front, re-creating the road until he gained the other side. Too bad for the poor fellow who happened on it next.

One rainy season, Dad slid off the road, embedding the truck in a bank. It was an especially good fix, with wet, claying mud caked around his tires. To make matters more interesting, Dad had the foresight to choose a place swarming with **mpazhi**, Zambia's army ants.

These critters have the fantastic ability to creep up one's pant legs and bite on cue, like a room full of karate students chopping all at once. I never saw the ants carrying walkie-talkies; they didn't need them. How they knew when to bite is still a mystery, but they had a knack for finding the tender places that required a full-tilt strip to locate.

So Dad hustled in the mud while Mom worked the clutch. And the biters made haste to hard-to-reach places. When the ants gave the signal, Dad disrobed like any good African, picking off the little suckers with hurried fingers.

I can still see him (in my imagination), a white man in red skivvies, hopping around in the middle of the road. I wasn't actually there, so I might have made up the red skivvies. Still it makes for a good story, and I like good stories.

Dad said that was the fastest he's ever gotten unstuck.

I couldn't say how many times it happened, but we got stuck more when we lived in the bush. For that reason alone, I recommend bush-living for any boy who gets to decide where he wants to grow up.

13

Zambian village life isn't exactly a study in exuberant colors. People wore what they had. To wear a 'matching outfit' meant one put on trousers *and* a shirt. That people in some countries even bothered trying to coordinate color, fabrics and prints didn't dawn on me until I got engaged.

Villages were like underpopulated neighborhoods joined by foot paths instead of heaped together in a city block. Each village was surrounded by its own fields. Most had a banana grove or two and huts situated wherever was the most convenient. If there was a deep cultural meaning to the placement of every shelter, I didn't know what it was.

The tones of earth and thatch worked in simple harmony with surrounding bush. Most Americans considered huts to be synonymous with poverty. I never saw them like that.

Split bamboo lashed into a lattice type wall plastered with a mixture of mud and clay made Africa's version of adobe. The walls kept out the heat, provided space for sleeping and occasionally offered an ante-room for a small table. Most living was done outside, the fringe benefit of having the best weather on the planet. Temperatures average 75 to 80 degrees Fahrenheit year 'round!

A well-thatched roof is a thing of beauty. Thick bundles of long-stemmed grass are laid atop a skeleton of rough-hewn poles cut from surrounding Miombo woodlands. Starting at the eves, grass bundles are tied to the poles with bark rope softened in water. The bark rope shrink as it dries, securely binding thatch to poles. Once a circuit is complete, the next and higher layer is added until the entire roof is under cover. A ridge cap of grass is sewn onto the peak to keep it dry. If a person plans to stay a while, the ends of the grass will be pushed up and in with a shaping tool until the first course meets the second. Then only the bottom ends are visible and the roof rises perfectly to the top.

Unlike a tin roof, eight to ten inches of thatch is a perfect insulator and keeps a hut cool under sub-tropical sun. Closely packed thatch remains relatively fire retardant because it burns as ineffectively as a closed phone book. Active sparks or smoldering sections are easily removed by cutting them out. The life span of a thatched roof rivals the best asphalt shingles, often lasting better than twenty years.

Considering the fact that the entire structure was accomplished without a single trip to a hardware store and constructed completely with locally grown, renewable resources, it's hard to find fault with the idea. Unless a man paid for the thatch, he probably managed the whole business at the cost of only his time. It's a long way from the term of indenture known as a thirty-year mortgage.

In the village, grass belonged on the roof, not on the ground. Open areas around huts were (in a twist of irony) daily swept clean with handle-less *grass* brooms. After all, bare, hard-baked ground is simpler to manage in the absence of lawn mowers. Ants, snakes and other unfriendlies are more easily deterred. Usually a bare necked, scrawny-legged chicken patrolled the open space, beady eyes on the sharp for grasshoppers and other meaty bits. The chicken coop was shaped like a miniature hut and constructed entirely of thatch suspended off the ground on long poles. A raised roost provided better protection in the night hours from rock pythons, jackals, caracal, serval, wild cats, and other creatures, all of whom went about in the dark.

Most villages had a kinzanza for visiting. These breezy shelters had a thatch roof with supporting posts but no walls. Mango trees served the same purpose, offering the luxury of a seasonal snack besides. A good host would not keep visitors in the sun.

Low, square goat-hide stools with patterns burned into the wooden legs provided visitor seating. Other stools, carved into elephants from chunks of ebony, bore the weight of a circular seat above them with upraised trunks and solid shoulders.

People who live deliberately connect deliberately. In Zambia, hospitality was the rule. An old man told me that as a child, he could have walked across the entire country and always have a meal and a place to stay when evening came. Funny that people with so little, relative to their blanched, rat-racing cousins, should know so much about generosity. I saw a full measure of poverty in Africa, but I saw more people happy to share whatever they had. The largesse of their hospitality puts the western world to shame and debunks the myth that wealthy people give more.

Zambia's people are the friendliest I have ever met. Maybe because so much of the country, at least at that time, traveled by foot. And people on foot have time to stop and talk a while.

Whether visiting with an axe-toting woodsman in the bush or an old woman tending maize on her brazier by the road, the offer for conversation was always open.

A Zambian bishop once told me that American's worship the god on their wrist (the watch). Time was something Americans were afraid to waste. The African, he explained, saw time as something to move through. Africa wasn't in a hurry.

Village life revolved around crops, and crops revolved around weather. Women pounded dried maize into flour to use for the staple meal, nshima. Her kina, or mortar, hollowed out from a single tree trunk stood upright. It, too, was carved and decorated with similar burning techniques as the stools.

Once the maize is ground, the meal is boiled with water, ever thickened until it can be rolled into bite sized balls and dipped in a vegetable side dish known as a relish. There's nothing like it.

Although my early picture of rural life in Africa might tend toward the idyllic, in reality, lives were governed by powers beyond control. Some lived in fear of a darkness more pressing than night and a tangible, spiritual evil. As such, the medicine man wielded considerable power. But his charms, amulets and potions brought no lasting peace or prosperity.

Children suffered the worst. The malaria parasite was responsible for the greatest human toll. Most everyone knew someone who had died from malaria. Some estimates suggest that every three minutes one child dies from malaria in Africa. If someone turned up at a clinic in America with malaria, they would probably be admitted. In Zambia, it was a case of "take your medicine and go to bed."

Though Dad and Mom suffered through several rounds of malaria, I managed to escape with not a one. Perhaps, due to the fact that I accidentally overdosed on the prophylactic (malaria preventative), or because of a natural resistance.

Maybe I just taste bad.

While the intermittent use of a mosquito net didn't hurt, it was more likely just the kindness of God and a hyper-vigilant guardian angel with a fly swatter.

14

Sakeji School

1982

When I returned to Sakeji, my mosquito-net kingdom stayed dry.

I'm sure the laundry ladies were glad. All the laundry at the Sakeji School was washed on the rocks by the river by village women and laid out on grass to dry. Laundry day for one hundred children made quite a display, what with all that European clothing spread out under the African sun. But the women laughed and talked and sang while they worked.

My new bed nested in an alcove by the window. I'd moved up a room, further away from the head master's apartment. I had no big brother assigned to me. I shared the alcove with Samuel Logan, David Mpumba, and Christopher Rough. Maybe others. I can't remember now.

Located in a distinctly sub-tropical zone, rainy season thunder cracked so close it made the ground shake. My bed, set by the window, gave the perfect spot from which to count lightning strikes. It was not uncommon for me to fall asleep after reaching seventy. The brilliant momentary invasions into Africa's inky darkness left spots on my eyes and birthed a wonderful rain-smell that drifted through screened windows.

Most Sakeji kids hold a sentimental love for the song of rain on a tin roof. Storms gave opportunity for kids to talk and sing as loud as they wanted after lights-out. The rain hammered so hard on the corrugated roof that it drowned out every other sound. The pounding stopped suddenly, as only a tropical storm can, and someone had to shush the kids who hadn't noticed.

During the day, rain splashed on our legs as we ran from the dining hall to class. Torrents collected in rivulets, gathering strength and muddy earth from the parade ground on its way to the Sakeji River.

When it wasn't raining, the area beyond school property offered a perfect playground for young explorers. At times we'd head out as groups of boys with Miss Hoyte on a hike, racing ahead down the trails, hemmed in on either side by stands of grass too tall to see over.

Other times, when all the kids played at the Sakeji River, special permission from a teacher could be procured to head out of bounds. The bush around Sakeji grew thick and deep. Wild fruit waited for those who knew where to find it. Following typical African footpaths, we forged into the bush, hunting fruit. Some we named by the color of the peel. Leopards and lions had a tough skin with slippery seeds on the inside. The seeds sloshed around in our mouths as teeth stripped the pulp before the whole business was discarded in one fantastic mess.

Closer to the river we found shindwa. These grew underground, revealing only the top end of their thick red peel. I suppose it was a flower bulb. Roughly triangular pods came to an uncertain point at each end, vaguely resembling a too-short, squat banana. A shindwa had to be opened with your teeth. Biting down on the corners popped open the sides enough that the tough peel could be removed and the super-sour mass of white pulp and black seeds gobbled up in one delicious mouthful. Shindwa seeds are probably the *grains of paradise*, an ancient substitute for pepper and sometimes-additive to strong drink. While the seeds may have been caravanned across the Sahara to northern markets, we knew nothing of their history and found them along the river banks, not far from the source of the

Great Zambezi River. To us, they were simply sour candy God made for Sakeji kids.

The river and nearby trees offered my favorite recreation and filled rare free-time and half-term breaks. Because of the distances involved, kids didn't go home for half-term.

Trees not only provided recreation, they afforded us an unusual liberty. Climbing a tree took me out of the world of head masters and dormitories. Teachers never climbed. It wasn't, I suppose, the sensible, "British" thing to do. The higher, denser and more difficult trees became our 'upper room.'

One group of boys worked out a series of agility and climbing obstacles to serve as an initiation test for others who wanted to join their troop. The Monkey Gang was born. Difficult trees had to be ascended, obstacles conquered. Walk up one tree. Leap across to another.

I managed to pass the entrance exam and join the ranks. As best as I remember, Jason Carpenter, Ian Frew, Martin Kemp and a few others were my tree-brothers. Monkeys, hanging from our clubhouse.

Big stuff for an eight-year-old.

Like baboons, we'd make forays to terra firma to play and hunt for fruit. We built a small rock dam on the Sakeji River and rigged a fish hook on five inches of line from a branch. We left the branch wedged in the rocks and were rewarded with a slippery catfish the next day.

Most kids at the river knew where to get wild gum. We'd pluck the nub off a young tree, chew it past the bitter stage and spit it out before it began to dissolve.

The Monkey Gang traded with the village kids across the Sakeji River. Matchbox cars for wild fruit. Black market food. No pun intended. Once we smuggled a plastic bottle full of fruit to and from the dorm and ate them well after the expiration date. Of course, expiration dates were determined by the sniff test. Ripe. Over ripe. And wine.

15

The cost of working as a missionary in Africa, then, was pretty high. In taking us to school, Dad and Mom joined the class of people who paid dearly for their mission. Back home, Dad and Mom re-entered their normal routine, pushing past the too-early empty nest. Teaching classes, visiting churches and homes while managing the stuff of every-day life that took ever-so much longer than in the States.

Boarding school wasn't easy for anyone.

Sakeji was operated and staffed mostly by conservative British missionaries who, by God's grace, determined to make sensible British children out of us all. One morning Mr. Foster marched the entire school body into the Hall where we sat, as usual, on the concrete floor in straight lines. A knife, fork and spoon protruded from the breast pocket of his blue checked shirt.

"The knife is held in the right hand. The fork in the left." He mimed eating in the air. Eating correctly was serious business. The only right way, after all, was the British way.

I still don't eat well sans a knife. Feels like trying to dress without underthings.

Mr. Foster explained the appropriate way to eat soup, tipping the bowl away from oneself so as not to eat like an American or other uncivilized peoples on the earth.

He didn't say that. But the undercurrent among kids at Sakeji was the same. Self-identifying as 'American' in Zambia wasn't exactly a perk, Americans being widely regarded as loud, gum-chewing, cultural illiterates. They were a spoiled and under-civilized people. One day, maybe, they might rise to the level of the British, but it was still too early in the game to call.

Miss Halls was Head Mistress. She was as imposing and frightening a person as Mr. Foster.

She, too, was appalled at the shocking lack of decorum and polish. Taking Mr. Foster's lead, she marched us into the Hall on another day to demonstrate the proper use of a hanky. The constant sniffing, snorting, and hocking during cold season had driven her to the very brink, and we were to learn how to use a hanky, or else. The hanky was as essential a part of our daily uniform as the knee-high socks folded over elastic bands above our calves. A flaccid sock about one's ankle had no place among such cultured people.

Miss Halls stood in front of the entire student body, unveiled her hanky and demonstrated the perfect nose blow, pressing first one nostril, then switching sides to vacate the other cavity. The damp mess was folded and tucked back into the sleeve of her cardigan. Boys had pockets.

At her direction, every single child withdrew their hanky. With military precision, we followed Miss Halls through a rigorous real-life drill. One-hundred and ten children blew their nose in unison.

Quite a sound.

Black Africans had an ever-so-much-better solution. Their method involved holding one nostril closed and turning one's head to the side, followed by a rapid explosion of wind to carry snot from their noses out into the grass. Should a residual ribbon of mucus stick to their nose, a simple wipe-off with a twig would complete the sterile procedure. They took their turn to wonder at the British barbarians who collected such rubbish from their sinuses and tucked the mess away for safe keeping!

At recess, we practiced the African method. Leaning over, we blew strings of yellow snot, competing for the longest unbroken rope. We became firemen, dousing imaginary flames. Strings of snot swung from our noses. We blew until our faces got red and ears popped. I don't remember who won. Besides, they probably wouldn't want me to mention it. That kind of thing only makes one famous at eight years of age.

A British run boarding school in post-colonial Africa presented a host of paradoxes. Sakeji was a melting pot, a microcosm of the great American experiment, set in one of the planet's most obscure places. On nationality day, kids lined up by nation of origin which was always a bit confusing for me. Although I carried an American passport, I had a Zambian birth certificate and Dad might have applied for his Zimbabwean citizenship. Furthermore, it wasn't exactly a perk to be American. Americans had, after all, rebelled against the Crown, dumped perfectly good tea into the sea and generally made a nuisance of themselves around the world, acting like they know how to run everyone else's country. Most of the time Julie and I were lumped in the American line, which I suppose makes sense and no sense at the same time.

Sometimes there were as many as twelve different lines. Some 'came' from Australia, Denmark, New Zealand and the United Kingdom. Others hailed from Canada, the United States, or Zambia (white *and* black, if you're curious). There were more countries represented, but I've forgotten them now.

White children of landowners, farmers mostly, got to stand in the Zambian line, though somewhere in their past *someone* came from somewhere else.

Maybe if you own land in a place, that's the ticket to belonging. But follow that line of reasoning for a few minutes and it will soon come to pieces like bread in milk. I dare you to find a non-land owning American and tell him he's got no business calling himself a U.S. citizen.

Most of the time, kids don't care where you're from. We shared the same space, played the same games, ate the same food and scratched out our lessons with pens dipped in the same ink wells.

16

Yes. Ink wells. Honest-to-goodness pots of ink wherein one dips the quill. Only we didn't use quills. Far too advanced for that. We used a calligraphy pen. Dip, blot, write a few words, and dip again before the letters start getting pale.

I stared at the cursive sentences chalked on the black board. Miss Halls wrote on, oblivious to my complete ignorance of cursive. It looked pretty but was complete nonsense. Somewhere between my first and third year in school, I had missed the lesson where kids learn to decode the stuff. I panicked. How was I supposed to follow along when I couldn't read the board? How many times could I ask, "Miss Hall, what's that word?" when every word was cipher?

I tightened my grip and pressed harder. More ink can be milked from a regular ball-point pen (biro) by pressing harder. Not so with these jobs. Metal tips bend and bow and spread and soon it's all over. I tried to bend the tips straight. It gave me a permanent ink stain on my fingers.

The chalky words swam on the board. I whispered an s.o.s. to a nearby student, but only a fool would speak in Miss Halls class. I made more mistakes and scribbled them out. The scribbles turned into inky tar pits on my paper. Miss Halls stopped by.

"Just draw one line through the word to cross it out," she said.

But if I did *that*, then she'd still be able to see what I fool I'd been. Better to make the mistake disappear altogether. Obliteration. Annihilation.

I was censored for frequent tar pits.

We used those same pens to write letters home. Which were also censored.

Not that it mattered. Young kids can't write letters. Letter-writing day meant we'd sit in the classroom and copy phrases from the blackboard. "How are you? I am fine. We went to the river yesterday." The same stuff every time.

I can't imagine how desperate my folks must have been for real news. Or maybe I can.

Even if we had complete literary freedom, how does a six-year-old explain that he thinks he is dying? How can an eight-year-old plead for his parents to *please* come and take him home?

Mail-call was the best of times. Letters from home!

Kids gathered around the headmaster's apartment as he rifled through the pile, calling out names. Siblings gathered in knots on the parade ground to read their mail. I stood next to Julie, full of hope. Letters from home were the only things that mattered in my world. They made us want to find a private place to be sad and alone and with our parents at the same time. Little fingers worked open the same paper they had touched. Usually it had been too long in the mail to smell like them anymore. In the early years I couldn't read anyway, so I sat with Julie under the mango tree. Julie's face got blotchy when she read. It happened when she was going to cry. And I'd ask, again, how long until we went home.

Letters made home feel real. And they chronicled the story of a life apart.

Some kids always got letters. Some didn't. I remember their faces.

Wild fruit can be shared. Sakeji fudge can be shared. You can take turns on a skateboard. But you can't share a letter from home with someone who didn't get one. It didn't work. It didn't help.

I remember who I saw that day turning away with that angry, hurt, forgotten feeling. It bled up from his heart and onto his face. The boy who would soon break into manhood. But I won't say his name. Hurt like that is too deep to call out. That hurt that doesn't go away by itself.

Mail-call was the worst of times.

Thursday afternoon rally was the Boarding School version of Boy Scouts. We'd dress in our special uniform complete with a blue sash.

Standing at attention we'd recite in unison, "Honor all men; love the brotherhood, fear God, honor the king. First Peter chapter two verse seventeen." Though I was never certain, I figured it was the British King to whom we owed our allegiance. Being around Brits gave one the distinct impression that Sakeji School fell firmly within the King's dominion.

I didn't know England only had a queen.

The unstated goal of rally was to earn badges. Badges could be had for knot-tying, verse recitation, water rescue and flag semaphore. Flag semaphore was part of the maritime tradition and served as a means of telegraphy at sea. A flag in each hand was held at different positions to represent numbers or letters. Knowing the code, I suppose, meant the difference between life and death at sea.

I've not yet figured out why this system was of import in Zambia, a landlocked country without access to a single, blessed ocean. If someone 'over there' was in trouble, I'd just ankle it over and find out what it was.

Never mind. There I go, trying to make sense of something.

17

Oral tradition thrived at Sakeji. Stories were handed down from parents who attended the school, or passed along by upper grades. Even ink wells had stories. Dad kept a bush baby when he was at Sakeji. These miniature monkeys with round black eyes and tiny fingers fit comfortably in the palm of one's hand. Dad's bush baby went to class in his shirt pocket and used the ink well in his neighbor's desk for a urinal. Ink-well holes in desk tops did look remarkably like a long-drop.

School records also survived by oral tradition. Who consumed the most rice cakes? Who swam the farthest underwater?

Dorms. Menus. Food. Nothing changed one stitch between the time Dad left in 1960 and when we showed up in the late 70's. Only the trees were bigger. In the sameness was a familiarity that connected us to family. A way of feeling close to those far away. It wasn't much, but it was something.

Every story Dad told me about Sakeji played out on a familiar stage. But most of *his* stories are forgotten. Forgotten in the haze of trauma or the after-effects of trypanosomiasis (sleeping sickness) delivered courtesy of a tsetse fly. He doesn't know which.

As I lay in my netted kingdom, the weight of missing Mom and Dad pressed in so hard I couldn't sleep. I lay awake keeping my inner eye focused on going home as if the end of term might not come if I didn't.

Miss Hoyt, the school nurse, walked into the boy's dorm and found me among all the others. I wasn't making noise. I wasn't crying aloud. But she found me and sat on the edge of my bed. She whispered through the mosquito net, telling stories of Dad and his brother, Tom. The twins. She remembered for me the time when Tim and Tom made a shortcut into his mosquito net by cutting a door in the side. The twins had a good time leaping through into their beds. Until they were caught.

Then it didn't go so well.

I think God told Miss Hoyt to come and find me. She pulled me out of the pit I was digging and tied the thread of my life back together with my family. It only happened once.

It was the only time I remember any adult tending to an individual emotional need.

God bless Miss Hoyt.

On the surface everything was fine. Kids played. We laughed. We kept busy. But underneath every day and every moment the acid of loneliness burned holes in our hearts. Most of mine have healed now. Others keep their hurt buried.

The sameness of Sakeji made me feel like I was reading Dad's journal. Not that he kept one, but there was comfort knowing he'd done this before. Knowing he'd survived.

Milo, one of the grounds keepers, had been around then, too. He must have had a stroke because he drooled constantly. Couldn't make his bottom lip stand up. Sometimes I went and sat near him to watch him work. Being with someone who had known Dad—though decades before—still felt like being closer to my family than nothing at all.

Dad recalled the haircuts. Ba (Mr.) Venus had a reputation and Dad mostly remembers the moles that got taken off when Venus used the horse hair clippers on his neck. We, too, lined up by Ba Venus under the same loquat tree to get our bowl cuts. Hideous looking whack jobs that made every boy's hair look remarkably uniform. Then out came the horse-hair clippers. And out came the memories.

On the parade ground kids still played marbles and flushed crickets from their earthen holes and gave them to local staff to cook. Just like Dad, I caught them. As big as my hand and not much to look at. Unlike Dad, I never ate one. I never got that hungry.

The ritual of Sakeji fudge came on Sunday after lunch. Two crunchy, square pieces, gritty from unmelted raw sugar. Slices of heaven. Leftover fudge sometimes made it into our candy tins. Most times not.

I was never any good at saving fudge.

Once I attempted to give a piece to Catherine Moffat. She was my girlfriend, even if we almost never talked. My gift started out square, but the edges were uneven, so I nibbled them off. Then the corners. Pretty soon it was almost round. And getting smaller. We met by the playground before supper. All I had left was a puck-shaped piece. I gave it to her.

She gave me hers. Still square. Untouched. Untasted. I was ashamed.

But I still remember her gentle kindness. Little kindnesses go a long way in prison.

18

Before children's church, the younger grades lined up to file into the Hall. Once inside, we sat on the concrete in tidy lines while Miss Hall led a hymn. One Sunday close to Christmas, she looked over her piano and bifocals and called out the hymn number for Away in a Manger. "And Dwight," she added, ever-so-matter of factly, "will stand up and sing the second verse as a solo."

Just like that. No warning. While the rest of the kids sang the first verse, I had plenty of time to work up a full-blown case of pre-song jitters. The second verse wound down. I stood, resigned, not given a choice in the matter.

Lines of faces stared, thrilled they hadn't been chosen.

Miss Hall must have known my parents sang. Maybe she assumed the ability had rubbed off or been inherited. I don't rightly know.

Sunday evenings, David Mpumba, a few other kids and I gathered around the Hall piano and read over Miss Halls' shoulder while we belted out our favorite hymns. I did love to sing. I made her play *The Old Rugged Cross* every time. The cross at the center of that song was at the center of my life, too.

But I wasn't prepared for my musical debut.

Chapped knees threatened to buckle, feeling like they belonged to someone else. My lungs pumped air uselessly in and out, filling my head with a light-fuzziness. Somewhere in the far distance, Miss Halls pushed on, playing the opening bars of the second verse.

A thin, clear voice rose from inside, quivering slightly, stumbling here and there. I pushed on, straining against the horrible honor of it until I reached the end and collapsed back into my place.

With so many children and so few adults, I lived under the assumption that I wasn't noticed. Miss Halls' unwelcome invitation to sing assaulted that premise.

Though I was never again required to perform an instant solo, I was tasked with one for the end-of-year play.

Little boy kneels at the foot of his bed, droops on his little hands, little gold head.

Hush, hush, whisper, who dares. Christopher Robin is saying his prayers.

Thus began my journey of becoming comfortable in front of people. I still like to sing, but to this day, regardless of group size, I would rather speak for an hour than sing for a minute.

19

Sakeji School

1983

I came *close* to a real paddling a few times at Sakeji. That is to say, I'm either an exceptionally lucky fellow, very good, or just plain clever.

I like the clever bit.

(I *might* have had a few more spankings at home. The folks say I had a stubborn streak. I'm sure I have no idea what they're talking about.)

Afternoon rest time was strictly observed for younger grades. A few slept, the rest whispered, careful to stay in bed when the monitor was around. At the first sound of the monitor or Head Master, someone whispered an urgent "chips," and we'd go scrambling back to our places, assuming what we believed was the perfect been-here-all-the-time posture. The monitor was one of the older boys tasked with keeping us in check. Any child found out of bed or talking was sent into the hallway. Several steps from death row, those in the hall sat with backs to the wall, and eyes on the Head Master's flat. Because we had no doors, we watched them waiting for it. If and when the Head Master entered the dorm, every child in the hall got a simple corrective whack to the backside. Mr. Foster just worked his way down the grim line, paddling the frequent fliers harder than the rest.

Assembly-line spanking.

Sitting there with breathless uncertain anticipation, some boys probably found the experience satisfied a primal need similar to a round of Russian Roulette. I didn't spent much time in the hall. It was my clear aim to avoid punishment at all costs. Be it shame or a fear-based aversion, I cannot say.

I have no primal needs of that kind.

The few times I was sent to linger in the hall, seconds froze into minutes. My eyes glued to the dreaded Head Master's door, willing it to stay closed. A spanking from a stranger was completely untenable.

Thankfully, the hall monitor also had rights to dismiss boys back to their beds at will. I suppose my pastey white face and panicked eyes did the trick. At a nod, I dashed back to bed, breathless with relief and resolved to remain on the safe side of the law.

In fact, aside from the well-deserved ruler-to-knuckle smack from Miss Ross, I managed to escape the paddle entirely. Almost.

Into every life a little rain must fall.

Because of the number of children, birthdays are not celebrated on the day. The school hosted one birthday party for those who passed their milestone that term. It was a blast. For once, teachers lowered their guard and sugar flowed freely. Kids put on skits. The celebrated ones—in a shocking affront to all that was proper—*stood* on their chairs and were showered with song and a few 'hip-hip's from the Head Master himself. The rest of the students hoorayed with gusto.

A group of us performed the "Ugliest Man" skit. The Head Master—as if he were suddenly a friend—was led out of the dining hall while *the hideous one* (me) stood under a blanket on stage at the front of the dining hall. One of the players filed up to the blanket, peeked underneath and dropped dead at my feet, overcome by the ugliness.

Another kid sauntered up, peeked underneath and died a dramatic death. Then another. Anticipation grew.

At last, the Head Master was brought back in after the dead bodies had been dragged to the side. Unaware of the prior vignette, he was instructed to look under the blanket.

As soon as I saw his face, I dropped dead at his feet. The Head Master, knowing he had somehow played the fool, stood sheepishly holding the blanket's edge. I thus conferred the title of "Ugliest Man" to the one I most feared.

The skit resulted in an instant uproar from the children.

There was a kind of fantastic karma in all of it. We *actually* pulled one over on the Head Master.

Under the influence of a successful skit and the general uncorking of all our child-like exuberance, I returned to the dorm on a high.

Miss Hoyte and Miss Eastbury, God-bless them, had the thankless task of corralling the troop of stampeding boys and herding them to bed. However, shouldering up at a common urinal presented the perfect time to play fireman, standing as far back as possible from the target in an attempt to outdistance each other.

Miss Eastbury appeared out of nowhere. She was not impressed and completed her own hasty version of assembly-line spanking.

Grabbing us by our shoulders, she planted a firm whack, rapid-fire on several backsides with the result that our fire hoses turned into sprinklers. In the heat of the moment, Miss Eastbury failed to consider exactly what might happen to a boy-child's water during a spanking.

It didn't exactly hurt, but it was rather messy.

That sprinkler-spanking turned out to be the worst I got.

I will add that spanking was a normal part of my upbringing. But having Dad lay me over his knee was different than the corporal punishment administered in a context like Sakeji where no relationship existed with the Head Master.

I never remember a time Mom and Dad spanked in anger. And every one of their spankings was followed by long snuggle times where I was reminded I was loved. There was a kindness in their correction to which I (eventually) responded. A swat on my hinder was kinder than the end result of making a pathway out of rebellion.

The eternal sameness at Sakeji changed after I left. Ceilings were added to the dorms. Pictures were hung. Colors changed to make it warm and friendly. But while the concrete floors may still have been polished with Cobra wax, the sense of connection and heritage had been broken.

I never visited Sakeji after I left, so in my memory, it is just like it always was.

According to family stories, the changes precipitated a disgruntled younger cousin of mine to do the unthinkable. (Sean was one of Aunt Cathy's kids.)

He had the guts to do what my heart always longed to do. Sean ran away from school.

He's a surgeon now. A smart guy. Desperation inspires the improbable. White skin has more than once proven to be a distinct disadvantage. White boys can't hide.

They found Sean. It was a simple case of the Head Master driving down the road and asking the first villager he came upon, "Have you seen a white boy going this way?"

"Yes, bwana. He went that way."

Sean should have tried a leopard skin.

20

The Sakeji library smelled of ink and old paper. The wooden racks held volumes collected over the fifty years the school had been in operation. Names scrawled with pencil on library cards tucked into the back pocket of every book cataloged the students of days gone by. Their names marked with elementary handwriting made time stand still in the library.

Daydreaming didn't help the intolerable waiting, but I often stood at the library window and looked out onto the road. I imagined Mom and Dad driving up the hill to get me.

There was something else in that library. Or Someone else. I felt it but didn't pay attention. A Presence watched me. Waited for me, offering me a Father's comfort. But I didn't want Peace in my circumstances, I wanted the circumstance to change.

But eventually it would happen. The days wound down and the end came into view. I started to breathe again.

At the end of term, parents gathered at the river to wait. Kids were not officially released until after rest time on the last day of term.

The parents socialized, pretending not to watch the clock. As the allotted time grew closer, the dads moved surreptitiously toward their vehicles and soon pandemonium broke loose as they scrambled for position in the parade of cars set to drive up the hill to collect their children.

The first car got to set the pace up the single dirt lane. Traditionally, it traveled as slow as possible, creeping up the hill while the kids at the top crowded outside the dining hall shouting "mush," full-to-bursting with anticipation. David Salisbury, one of Dad's Sakeji classmates, was the worst when he made the front of the line. I didn't think anyone *could* drive that slow. He was a man with a lead foot any other day. The parade of parents behind hooted and carried-on, and he'd crawl forward, pretending he was the only person in the world, late for nothing and stopping frequently to let ants cross the road. He ignored the blaring horns and rumble of diesel engines to drag out the fantastic excitement of term's end.

If the lead driver was one of those tear-off-the-wrapping-paper sorts, the line of cars charged up the hill, looking like a low-budget, missionary, bush rally. When Dad made the front, he drove like a mad man. As soon as we got them out of the truck we'd be hugging and laughing and trying to forget how long it had been, how much it hurt and how many weeks of break stood between us and the next term.

At the end of term, our parents bunked down wherever they kept them overnight before we made our return journey. My friends and I finally screwed up enough courage to escape prison and go exploring.

We talked about these escapades far in advance, planning every move. There was a group of us determined to test our mettle against the system. Someone made sure the bathroom windows were left open a crack.

We slipped to the end of the dorm after most boys had gone to sleep, drawn by a chance to bring to fruition the dream of breaking out. Not that it mattered at the end of term. We were leaving anyway. But it was the principle of the thing. We needed to prove we were free.

One by one we dropped through the window, keeping low to the ground. The Assistant Head Master's house was just off the end of the boys' dorm. It looked quiet. We crouch-ran to the playground where we huddled, checking to make sure the coast was clear. The few light bulbs didn't penetrate the darkness.

Then the unthinkable happened. Mr. Brubaker opened his door and stepped into the night, panning his torch *(flashlight)* like a giant light saber. We hit the dirt, burying our heads under hands. Yet again, being a white boy wasn't helpful.

We lay, silent as the grave. The long white arm of law continued to shark through the darkness as he walked from his house, probably to turn off the generator. Once the students were in bed, the need for power disappeared. We waited, breathless, until the light danced its way past us.

At last we stood and crept around the tennis courts to the back of the Hall. Darting inside, we congratulated each other for not getting caught. The inside of the hall yawned with its own emptiness. Every whisper and rustle of clothing bounced around carelessly in the brick and concrete. Moving more by feel than sight, we found our way to a row of tables still set up from the parent's reception. Impossibly, there were platters of leftover biscuits (cookies). We began to fill our pockets, guiltily grabbing handfuls of loot. What fortune!

One of the boys, beside himself with greed, bumped a tin platter onto the concrete. The hollow hall erupted with noise.

We ran over ourselves in our flight from the echo chamber. Five pajama-clad boys, giggling with fear and adrenaline, sprinted barefoot across the grounds, hoping against hope we didn't bump into the Assistant Head Master. Sure that we were running seconds ahead of the paddle, we made good our escape through the window and into the shelter of the dorm.

It wasn't my only venture to the outside, but it was the most memorable.

The truth is, I was too afraid of getting paddled to try it any other time of the year. Dad probably escaped more when he was at school.

But then, he got in trouble more than I did.

21

May 1984

We spent our next term break in town because Mom and Dad had moved back to Ndola to work at the Theological College of Central Africa. The drive from Sakeji in the farthest corner of the Northwestern Province took ten to twelve hours, depending on road conditions.

Ndola sat in a line of cities known as the Copperbelt. It grew up around a mining industry which fueled economic development and the spread of a mystery disease that eventually came to be known as AIDS. The city rode the mining boom or bust, depending on the price of copper shares on international markets. Zambian towns didn't stand out with sky scrapers as they are wont to do in the West. Brick and mortar retail stores projected as much warmth as a prison tuck shop. Here and there, in open spaces, tailors bent over shining trundle-powered Singer sewing machines, the needle snickering happily up and down. White haired, dusty, old men played games under the thick shade or brilliant display of a mango, red flamboyant or purple jacaranda tree. Wrinkled fingers moved checkers, pitting orange Fanta bottle caps against rusty Coca-Cola caps.

Outside the city proper, townships sprawled with names I've now forgotten. Here housing took the eclectic and haphazard shape of most urban slums in the developing world. The rutted roads cutting through them swam with foot traffic and the ubiquitous black bicycle. Pedestrians avoided gutters running with filth or rainy-season puddles which stretched across the entire road. Mud brick squared off against less fortified structures quilted together from plastic and tin. Metal drums, cut open and hammered flat conspired with rough cut poles carried in from the bush to provide chaotic and ineffective shelter.

Open-air markets hosted mounds of local wares. Pieces of cloth and grass mats on bare earth served as less complicated displays for piles of sweet potatoes, over ripe tomatoes, peppers, mangos and pawpaws. The sickly rot and reek of fruit and unwashed humanity drew flies that crawled unmolested over tomorrow's meal. And around it all, people called and laughed and greeted and haggled to create the marvel of the African township.

I so love Africa.

While there were a few multi-story buildings, almost all the houses in established neighborhoods were single-story block homes with corrugated roofing. Rectangular openings for ventilation along the eaves of a house were screened over to keep insects from using them as a through-way. Iron-framed windows hung behind security bars welded out of reinforcing bar. Some had an ornamental flair, others were purely utilitarian.

The prevalence of theft in town dictated iron bars, chain-link fences and block walls with broken glass mortared into the top. We owned dogs for security reasons, not pleasure.

Hence, Cindy and Bimbo, Doberman and German Shepherd respectively.

Soldiers sporting automatic weapons, manned frequent security check-points all across the country. The line of sandbags indicating a check-point looked more like they belonged in East Berlin before glasnost. The sight of armed military police in green fatigues chatting with Dad and leaning casually in our truck window didn't bother me one fig, unless the man was drunk. Automatic weapons were just the furniture of my childhood. Sometimes Dad rattled off Kaonde at a checkpoint and the soldiers laughed to hear this white man prattling away in a tribal language.

Ndola's proximity to Zaire (now D.R.C.) provided thieves with a largely unguarded international border within a few minutes' drive. Most crime went unsolved, thanks in part, to a hugely under-staffed and under-funded force. Early on, police lumbered around in coughing Land Rovers or commandeered rides to the scene of a crime. No one was *ever* caught for speeding.

Thieves ransacked our house five times. On one occasion it looked like a disgruntled team of CIA agents had given the place an uncommonly good shakedown. I didn't own much. They didn't take my bike, so I wasn't rattled. By the time police arrived, the trail was cold and moss had started to grow. Reports were filed. Paperwork submitted. Nothing ever happened.

It wasn't the prospect of being attacked by a gang of armed robbers that kept me awake. It was the mosquitos singing in my ear.

22

Ndola

Shopping options in town were extremely limited. Before 1980, trade with Zimbabwe to the south was off because Zimbabwe was busy having a war.

Small wonder that Mom's cookbooks included recipes like "Butterless-Eggless-Milkless Cake."

I've included the recipe here just in case you don't believe me.

Cooking in Zambia, Copyright E.C.Z. 1986.

Butterless-Eggless-Milkless Cake

Boil the following ingredients in saucepan for 3 min:

1 c sugar	*1/4 t nutmeg*
1 c water	*1/2 t cinnamon*
2 c raisins	*1 T cocoa*
1/3 c lard	*1/2 t cloves*

Remove from heat. Cool before adding:

2 c flour into which 1/2 t baking powder has been stirred.

Then boil 1/2 c water and add 1 t baking soda. Mix all this together and bake at 350 until toothpick tests clean and cake shrinks from edges of pan.

Just about everything had to be purchased in specialty shops. The bakery made bread and Mom stood in line. The only white woman. She watched the baker cut individuals loaves from the superloaf, watched him drop bread on the floor and pick it up without ceremony. No problem. No one cared. Not even Mom.

It was bread. Besides, a body could stand in line for a while and then the bakery might run out. If you got bread, you were lucky.

Eggs were sometimes found at vegetable stands—sold by the egg.

Flour was hard to find. Mom headed to the mill and hope to get some before it sold off to the bakeries. It wasn't actually Grade A, all-white, American bread flour. Mom described it as 'grey.'

Butter was unavailable unless Dad or Mom found a local dairy or stopped by the Dairy Board, the government-controlled farm cooperative.

For cooking oil, one also had to stand in line. Actually *scoring* the coveted oil was a treat.

The *grocery* store—something of a misnomer here—might *occasionally* have toilet paper. Usually not. Often the shelves were lined with non-perishables. Hoes. Enamel plates. Chinese made toys. Pillows. Peanut butter, *if* they had it, came in one variety. Like it or not.

Who needs a pillow when you have to stand in line for bread and vegetable oil? Who cares about toys when you're running low on toilet tissue?

Powdered milk is fine if you live on the moon. The most remote peoples of Mongolia turned their nose up at the stuff. Mom spooned the white powder into a Tupperware® mixer and gave it a good shake to get all the lumps out. If powdered milk is all you know, it's tolerable. Once the real stuff arrives, the substitute pales.

Mom was eventually able to buy fresh milk from a farm just out of town. The dairy operation was developed by a group of Danish farmers and pasteurized milk blew away the powdered substitute I was weaned on. I like to think that lack of (real) milk is responsible for my towering stature. At five-foot-eight, *tall* has never been one of my problems.

Our pantry always had Marmite. It is, I'm told, an acquired taste. But then, so are some people I've met. I don't know where we purchased our supply, but we never went without.

The black Marmite spread comes in a matching jar. Its yellow label unashamedly asserts itself as a Vitamin B extract, which means nothing at all to me. Though it has the color of tired automotive grease, the pithy, salty brilliance of it probably earned an apothecary a Nobel Prize.

As far as Marmite is concerned, watching someone try it for the first time pulls a close second to eating the stuff.

A few find it passable. Others find it impossible. Not that I enjoy, necessarily, seeing other people puke or spit, but, try as I might, the humor of it takes hold, and I can't keep myself from shaking with laughter. It's just funny.

I don't rightly know how a company like Marmite has managed to stay in business for over a hundred years with such a clear battle line between the Marmite lovers and the Marmite haters. Our family landed squarely in the love camp and have never left.

Local vegetable growers came to the front gate with tomatoes, eggplant and the like. Or should I say 'unlike.' I've never understood the eggplant. I *can* eat this creature, but I'd rather eat hippo or loquats or almost anything. I like hippo. I love loquats. I am not a fan of the slippery eggplant.

Thankfully, Mom pawned off our own garden-raised eggplant on a vegetable shop, though my folks liked it. Mom and Dad also wholesaled fresh pineapple they purchased from Sakeji ostensibly to use as 'ballast' in the truck on the way home.

Ballast? Pineapple?

Coffee, grown in Zambia, was purchased locally after 1980. Before that, Nescafe instant. Ricoffee was a local variation with chicory in it. Chicory was used as a coffee substitute in the Great Depression, World War II and during the East German coffee crisis of the late nineteen seventies. In other words, chicory wasn't ever in vogue as a flavor enhancer. That said, it must have fans because chicory-flavored coffee can still be had today at the finer Mediterranean-style cafes in Lusaka.

Ground corn meal, a staple food at *every* Zambian table was (almost) always available. Riots sometimes occurred when it wasn't. Once the riots got bad enough that the Zambian military deployed. Green helicopters thumped above the tree tops with gunners hanging out the side. Julie and I lay on the roof of the water tower to watch. Should we wave or not? Mom decided we should get down.

Just another day in paradise.

Once in a while, meat—usually turning various shades of green— was found in a grocery store, but only the brave bought it there. Better to find a local butcher, show up early, and hope to catch him with something left to sell.

Rice, like potatoes, peppers and other vegetables, was a seasonal crop.

Kapenta, a local dried fish not unlike sardines, stared out, eyes and all, from plastic bags with the tops tied shut. Weevils sauntered around under the plastic, happily getting a head start on it.

Exotic seasonings like salt, when available, came in unlabeled plastic bags, too. *When it was available.*

Chocolate? Not a chance. It was a different world.

But crates full of soda in glass bottles stacked beside rutted roads were purchased from local vendors. These purveyed their goods from discarded shipping containers converted to retail space. Coca-Cola, tonic water, Fanta, Sprite and lemonade.

Our own banana grove, guava, pawpaw and avocado trees provided the bulk of our fruit and Dad supplemented our meat diet by raising a warren of rabbits. Dad could hit, gut, clean and skin a rabbit in four minutes flat. Pretty good for a professor of theology.

Mom zazzed it up with whatever she had available.

23

Johannesburg, South Africa was our only reliable source for essentials like rice, flour, and salt. South Africa also had wine, cheese and chocolate! And it was a mere three-day drive.

With a distance roughly equivalent to traveling from London to Rome, or from Seattle to Los Angeles, it was quite a trip to a real grocery store.

Mom's signature, on-the-road breakfast was peanut-buttered toast stuck sticky side together and wrapped in a re-re-reused plastic bread bag. Once the toast was served, Mom and Dad embarked on that unique dance where Dad called out the pot holes and bumps so Mom could pour coffee from the green Stanley thermos without spilling. Julie and I bounced along in the back seat, watching the red African sun burn the dew off acacia trees. We'd make the four-hour drive to Lusaka the first day, then beat it for the Zimbabwean border on the next. The third day took us into Johannesburg.

Border crossings included the usual business of Africa's obsession with paper work, carbon copies and rubber stamps. Border agents gave our vehicle a perfunctory rummage, the thoroughness of this being determined by mood, curiosity or both. On one occasion, Mom and Dad stayed four hours at a border crossing while agents unloaded and checked every single bag, box and suitcase. After crossing the border, our trip south took us to the southern edge of the Zambezi escarpment and eventually across the Tropic of Capricorn.

In the 1970's, crossing Zimbabwe safely required official army escorts. Trucks with armed guards traveled in front and behind a convoy of vehicles. No one was allowed to stop until the procession passed the danger zones. When a government escort wasn't available, vehicles at the border crossing waited for a group and traveled together, at speed.

If traveling in Zimbabwe was too dangerous, we'd go through Botswana.

Zimbabwe came back to life after the war which ended in 1979. Her vibrant powerful economy, was driven, in large part, by the agricultural sector. The concept of commercial versus subsistence farming was a decidedly western idea and European farmers that immigrated to the country created an economy that flourished and provided employment for millions.

In Zimbabwe after the war, we'd get single-serve yogurt, plastic bags of milk and attend a movie, there not being many theaters in Zambia. I *did* go once to a Zambian theater and the experience was more like watching a sporting event. Viewers hooted, hissed and booed with as much passion as they might at a boxing match. It's a good time, if you like that sort of thing.

In Harare, Zimbabwe's capital, we'd stay with the Rea family (one of Dad's Sakeji chums) and enjoy their hospitality before continuing on to South Africa.

South Africa had a largely privatized economy where almost anything was available. The sanctions because of apartheid merely encouraged the development of local industry or trade with Asian countries who had fewer scruples.

Dad frequented Yusif, a friend and men's clothier, in Roodepoort, a suburb of Johannesburg. Yusif Said knew about hospitality. Though the colored community (mostly of Indian descent) had also been marginalized by the oppression of apartheid (South Africa's policy of racial segregation) they sensed a different spirit in my parents.

Dad and Mom knew how to relate to all kinds of people. I never thought much of it until later in life. Whether they were haggling with the bicycle grocer or chatting amiably with a soldier cradling his automatic weapon, my folks carried an uncommon grace to interact with people as people. They reached beyond the barriers of race, color, nationality, economic status and AK47's with humanity and kindness.

I've seen them interact with Afrikaaners over a backyard **braai** (cookouts) and dip their hands into communal dishes in rural villages. They grieved with their Zambian students over the loss of a child or laughed with the British about the silly things that make us different. They interacted easily with folks of any nationality.

There's something human about kindness, and honoring about greetings. Dad and Mom reminded us that the simple smile is understood in any language. They weren't afraid to touch people. Mom reached out to the women she was speaking with, bridging the residual gaps created by colonialism and paternalism with simple gestures. I saw Mom do it with ethnic Hawaiians who wanted to have fairer skin when the rest of the world was looking for a tan. I saw her do it in Portland, Oregon with people who had no idea how to cook a piece of elephant trunk.

The history of racism in any place is the story of distance. Distance between people and cultures, the powerful and the weak, races and genders, rich and poor.

Yusif welcomed us with ice-cold Cokes while Dad got measured up for alterations. The shop was alive with the smells of India and bolts of patterned cloth that, though Indian-made, were so distinctly African.

24

1984

Several of Dad's siblings worked in Africa for at least part of their career. Aunt Lois and her family left Zambia in 1975. Uncle Peter and his family moved to the Kingdom of Swaziland, four hours west of Johannesburg. The King of Swaziland, Sobhuza II passed away in 1982 after a more than eighty-two year reign—the longest reign of any monarch on record. He managed to marry seventy women and died with over one thousand grandchildren.

Dad's twin, Uncle Tom—who married only one woman—lived in Johannesburg, South Africa with their two children. He worked as a teacher and was involved with the Indian community in that area. South Africa offered more than a break from the scarcity and frustrations of living in Zambia, it also had my cousins. Matt and Lisa were roughly the same age as Julie and me. They provided an important link to an extended family that spanned across the globe. Matt and Lisa had been in the States in 1980 and we loved reconnecting in Johannesburg.

Our time together had, most of all, that warm feeling of being with relatives. Something that only happened intermittently.

That Sakeji term break was like any other. The complete bliss of waking up at home was like sunlight standing against the shadow of our pending return. As term break progressed, the dread of going back encroached and started to suck the joy away.

Julie had finished out her seventh year and last grade Sakeji offered. Uncle Tom called from Johannesburg offering an alternative. He suggested Julie and I live with them and attend day-school with Matt and Lisa.

Instead of being only twelve hours away by car, we'd be three days and two countries from home. We moved from a dorm of fifty, to a room with two. Lisa and Julie; Matt and Dwight. With no love lost on Sakeji, we faced the new alternative. But the biggest problem with Sakeji wasn't Sakeji. It was the absence of Mom and Dad.

I consoled myself with the thought of being near Uncle Tom, Dad's twin.

Yep, that's right. Dad is a twin and Mom is a twin.

It gets weirder. When Mom was a baby, Dad's grandmother, who lived in the Pacific Northwest, crossed paths with my mom's parents and asked to hold the twin girls. The year was probably 1948. Great-Grandma Kopp held Carol and Cathy Wilcox because her own grand-twins; Tim and Tom were in Northern Rhodesia (now Zambia).

A picture was taken.

The picture surfaced after Mom and Dad were married. Dad recognized the woman as his grandmother. It was one of those bursts of serendipity that gave the uncanny sense that Heaven had this in mind all along.

So Julie and I moved to South Africa. Mom and Dad drove us down. They stayed for a while and helped sort out the problem of school uniforms.

Grey shorts or trousers, white shirts and green ties. The tidy, grey knee socks were familiar enough, but it was the first time I had to wear a codified uniform. And the first time I had to tie a real tie.

Julie's summer uniform consisted of a pattered green dress complete with buttons up the front, white bobby socks and black shoes. In winter she wore a long sleeved white shirt under a green jumper (of the pinafore variety) and was subjected to a tie just like mine. Winter required the knee-high grey socks over black shoes.

Matching, natty, green blazers complete with the Discovery School emblem on the pocket finished us off.

The white residential areas of Johannesburg bore an uncanny resemblance to America's sleepy suburbia. It was surreal and perverse at the same time. The black townships looked nothing like them.

Schools for white kids were divided into South Africa's two white tribes. Afrikaner schools were conducted in Afrikaans (the Taal) with English classes taken from the earliest grades. Schools for students of British descent were in English with Afrikaans classes alongside. Afrikaners, of Dutch descent, first settled there in the 1600's.

This made my fourth school, if you're counting. My third educational system by the fifth grade, also known as Standard 3.

The first day of school, I stood behind my desk with a host of other boys and girls, greeting our teacher in unison before we were seated. Miss Williams, I think, was her name. She was probably the first teacher I ever had that felt approachable. She was young, kind and soft spoken. I'd been afraid of all other teachers without exception.

It didn't take much time before I was reading through the lines of her conversation to understand that she had no space for apartheid. Obviously the white community was divided on this front, and not just for reasons of simple bigotry, but it was good to know she had a different perspective.

In truth, as many (or more) whites despised apartheid as those who guarded it. But the rest of the world had every white South African pigeon-holed, wrapped, packed and labeled.

Her class was the first time I found an interest in history, learning about great explorers who first rounded the Cape. Men like Bartolomeu Dias and Vasco do Gama lived a world of adventure. They traveled beyond the known and it was, at least partly, their fault I had come to belong in black Africa.

Although Miss Williams' class felt safe, my academic world plummeted.

My primary aim was still surviving until the next term break when we would be reunited with our parents who lived thirteen hundred miles away.

The first day of Afrikaans class I followed someone down the breezy outdoor hallway, around the corner and into the room. Students remained standing at their desks, feet shuffling, until the teacher bid us good morning. My classmates chorused back, "Goeie More, Mevrouw Sweegis."

I was in a completely different Africa. Afrikaans didn't sound remotely like a Bantu language, which, at least as far as I was concerned, was easy to get my mouth around. I'd never seen so many awkward consonants in my life.

To make matters worse, group reading came next. Every student took a turn. The rotation got closer. Breathing got harder. How was I supposed to read this stuff?

I looked around. Whatever the kids were reading bore no resemblance to what I was seeing on the page. It's not like I hadn't heard Afrikaans before. But seeing the jumble of words on a picture-less page was another thing entirely. Now the reader was one row back. My eyes checked the desks beside me, hoping for a clue to where we were. Nothing.

The good Mevrouw stared me down. A nearby student leaned over and fingered a place on the page.

My turn? To read?

Why didn't she just throw me hieroglyphs instead? It might have been simpler.

So I began, listening to the silence as I groped hopelessly at the chaotic mess of letters. Unfortunately, this teacher knew all about giving students adequate wait-time. I thought she'd never let me go. My mouth worked its way around the consonants without making a sound, like a kid working his lips over a new set of braces. The silence of the room pulled like an over-stretched rubber band. At last something squeaked its way out. An attempt. My first word.

Complete rubbish.

The Mevrouw corrected me, I think. I had no idea what she was saying. It certainly bore no resemblance to what I was seeing on the page. I don't think she knew English. At least she wasn't sharing any of it with me.

I glanced around again, thinking maybe I was reading in the wrong place. Nope. They waited for me to keep going. I hated to interrupt what was, I'm sure, a gripping story, but instead sixty ears listened to this kid who had no idea how to read.

I embarked on the long journey of my second word, sick at the thought of an entire paragraph stretching out before me. This was going to take forever. Worse, this was only the first day of class.

Once again, I looked like everyone around me but was completely foreign.

All the kids at the Discovery School were white. By the time I showed up, they had already studied Afrikaans for five years. Immigrants (like Julie and me) were mainstreamed in language and given supplemental help in another class. Julie won the immigrant of the year award for her linguistic excellence.

I did not.

But by the end of my time in South Africa, I could say, "I don't speak Afrikaans" so perfectly I sounded like a complete liar, which I was not. All in all, I managed to learn a few important words, like 'shopping' and 'slippers' and 'peanut butter.'

Does not the world run on such things? Shopping, slippers and peanut butter?

It's **lekker**, eh?

Sotho, also a required language, was a bit easier, but it sounded far away from the Bantu languages on which my ears had been weaned. Sesotho, the official language of Lesotho, had somehow become part of the required curriculum of that all-white school and it suddenly became part of my early education.

It's not exactly a clear story line: Lost white boy from Zambia-America learns Sotho and Afrikaans.

25

The truth is that any two people who get together will struggle to communicate meaning.

If you can't relate, either you've never had friends, or you're dead. The varied languages of Africa paint a beautiful mosaic of cultural diversity. It also creates a few problems. The lingua franca isn't a panacea and communication challenges crop up even when speaking plain English.

Add to that the different word usage by various native-English-speaking 'tribes' and soon enough meaning gets muddled.

For example, an American might innocently compliment a Englishman's pants, not knowing he believes pants to refer to knickers, skivvies and under-drawers. A polite woman from New Zealand might pet a cat and coo, "nice pussy, nice pussy," having no idea the offense she's causing a nearby American. *Napkins* are sanitary pads to the English. Asking for a napkin to wipe your face sounds disgusting.

And Zambia hosts an antelope that is, when full grown, roughly the size of a jack rabbit. But one can scarcely mention the dik-dik without getting snickers from Americans.

To further illustrate this linguistic complication, Bimbo—whose name, though not our idea, was certainly fitting—needed his distemper booster. I tagged along while Dad trolleyed him off to the local vet. Bimbo, for all his hyper-activity, was a beautiful specimen of the German Shepherd. Even with the thirty-degree kink in his tail (the result of its being closed in a car door somewhere in the puppy years), Bimbo was a striking, and intimidating representation of the larger breeds.

We waited with Bimbo in the clinic's cool interior until the vet appeared. The doctor gave the animal a cursory glance and asked, "Is it a dog?"

I was gob-smacked. This man was a vet? What did he think it was? A camel? A shark. Egads! And we were going to allow this man to medicate our animal? He would probably draw the dose for a cow and kill it outright.

The man left, and I expressed my unstinting admiration for this veterinary 'genius.'

Dad explained. In England, a *dog* is a male. A female dog is a *bitch*.

I withdrew my hasty judgement, deciding my dog might live after all.

It wasn't my only veterinary run-in complicated by the English tongue. Almost twenty years later (also in Zambia), I had two cats destined to lose their manhood. The furry lumps needed prompt extraction before they sired all manner of feline descendants. But when I stopped by the clinic, the veterinarian was away. I left, being assured by the secretary she would contact me directly to schedule the procedure.

The call came. I answered.

The doctor—without smiling over the phone—said, "I've called to schedule your castration."

I swallowed hard. "Excuse me?"

"Yes. I'm calling to schedule your castration."

"Oh." I soldiered on, "I believe you've called to schedule the castration *for my cats…*"

An awkward silence ensued while I waited for the ambiguity to sink in. Nothing.

Communication can be a bitch.

26

My South African classmates had access to media, something we had little or nothing of in Zambia. I sat in the school library listening to the chatter of kids around me until someone mentioned a fellow named Michael Jackson.

They positively swooned.

Curious, I leaned back in my chair and asked, "Who's Michael Jackson?"

Mistake number one. Even libraries can get too quiet. Of all people, I knew the best way to stay invisible was to practice a strict regimen of 'nod-and-smile.'

"You don't know who Michael Jackson is?"

No idea. Too late to retract such a stupid question.

They stared, aghast, their faces frozen in absolute shock. Soon the room buzzed with the news.

Dwight didn't know about Michael Jackson. They knew I came down from Zambia, but what kind of an uneducated bushman was I?

EVERYONE knew Michael Jackson.

Everyone, I discovered, except me.

Culturally (at least as far as the arts were concerned), I was a Philistine. Michael Jackson hadn't invaded my world. We didn't have a television. In 1984, internet didn't exist. My Zambia had CocaCola, but not Michael Jackson.

Mr. Jackson had released *Thriller* the December before. His music video set records for international influence. As usual, I stood outside the winds of prevailing culture and completely out of touch with the rest of the world.

As life progressed, I sometimes stood outside on purpose, finding popular culture had no connection to my keyhole understanding of 'real life.' My frame of reference put music videos at impossibly odd angles to the stuff of everyday Africa. The people I knew had lives governed by demons and disease, crops and drought, life and death.

In my world, popular culture was irreverent and irrelevant.

Funny that I might one day write novels, contributing to 'popular culture.' One *can* look at the Mona Lisa through a peephole, but she can't be appreciated that way. Narrow world views are the same. Mine needed more Mr. Jackson to balance things out.

Michael Jackson drew people together in a way few other entertainers had ever done in the history of man. Any kid in America could have shared the enthusiasm of those kids in South Africa. Jackson created common ground, the beginnings of globalization.

In my case, the South Africa I stepped into bore no resemblance to the Africa I knew. The entire infrastructure, culture and economy of white South Africa functioned on a different planet.

My naiveté was extreme. I'd never heard a student swear in school until I got to South Africa. At least, never that I remember.

But I knew about people who lived in ways most of my classmates had never seen. I knew about animals and life and death and disease. I knew about being apart from people you love and the cost of it.

Michael Jackson couldn't help me with any of that.

27

But it was still Africa. One day Matt and I found a rhinoceros beetle. It looked like a gladiator dressed for the games. We added him to our collection of black widow spiders.

We needed to know who would win: The armored creature or the lithe poisonous one? Did I mention I was ten?

They met on the glass floor of a jam jar. We dumped the rhinoceros beetle into the jar where the black widow crouched, waiting.

We watched with the horrid fascination common to spectators in the Roman coliseum. The creatures battled, and we shivered with the heebie-jeebies when the black widow leapt onto the beetle's back.

The spider struck repeatedly but couldn't pierce the shell. The beetle's impressive collection of armor covered its entire body, but the spider continued to strike. Traumatized, the beetle marched endlessly forward, pushing his pronged trident against a glass wall he couldn't see and stumbling through the spiders net cast around his feet.

It was only a matter of time. Eventually, the spider found soft tissue beneath the beetle's helmet and sank her stingers between plates of armor. The beetle's body seized and slowed and the widow had the rhino for supper. One Jurassic meal with the audience of two bulging-eyed boys reeling with goose bumps and an unaccountable case of the willies.

Matt had an infectious thirst for fun that inspired us to all manner of crazy.

I still think it was his idea to hold the thermometer over the toaster, so we could feign a fever and stay home from church.

Toasters get hot.

The thermometer exploded. I took the heat. We went to church.

In South Africa, I no longer felt like the minority. Black Africans were only permitted in white neighborhoods if they had special permission to work as maids in white homes.

One day I walked along a narrow sidewalk toward an elderly black woman. I stepped aside out of deference, so she wouldn't have to walk in the wet grass. Respect for one's elders is a solid timber in the construct of African society. She immediately stepped off the sidewalk and stood still. I urged her to go ahead, but she chastised me, saying that I was just going to make trouble for her. What if someone saw her? Someone who didn't think white boys should honor their black elders.

A new contrast entered my experience. Another collision of cultures, ideas and ideals. I felt the cost of it everywhere. Shame lingered in shadows. Tension hid behind government policies.

Uncle Tom and Aunt Bonnie interacted frequently with the Indian South African population in and around Johannesburg. These, too, lived under the sting of apartheid, representing another 'colored' people—a group more or less separate and distinct from black Africa. Of course, they belonged just as much as anyone. Many had been in the country for generations and their homes represented yet another cultural piece set on the chessboard of my life.

Apparently, Indian South Africans show honor to a guest by making their curry extra hot. Compared to the mild-mannered (bland) nshima of Zambia, this was like eating fire. Though delicious, the heat crept from my mouth until my lips buzzed with pain and tears streamed from my eyes. The method was different, but they also ate with their fingers (like Zambians), making me feel right at home.

The Indians' attention to fabric and color and beauty was, to me, distinctly *other*. Where a village smelled like sweat, earth, grass and maize beer, the exotic smells of India joined a chaotic combination of spice, incense and dhal. I loved the smell of curry. Here the women wore their gold out loud and sometimes saris slipped to reveal trim brown midriffs or rolls of fat. The household idols sat squarely in their special places where a family focused their efforts to appease the angry gods, stave off disaster or curry favor. (Pun intended.)

Like buying insurance.

Not only did the racial segregation of apartheid fly in the face of everything I had known of Africa up to that time, but living with another family brought a daily reminder that I was not at home. The day-to-day drill had less structure than a hyper-scheduled boarding school. The adult-to-child ratio had fallen dramatically. Instead, I faced a family that lived in a 'normal' I neither felt nor could enter into.

Life apart from my parents was endured at best.

I suppose it is how people feel who have lost a loved one. They may continue in their routine, but the world around them swirls on, oblivious to the horror of their pain. People interact, laugh, play, shop, drive, and work in another reality. One doesn't wear a sign about one's neck proclaiming the loss. What good does it do to explain?

But sometimes worlds collide. A veil is torn and your reality leaks to the other side. Or another's reality comes through.

In most cases, the crossing over happens when someone reaches out, touches your pain and understands. That simple understanding bridges the gap between loss and regular life. When I found those people, it was as if the echo of my hurt resonated in their own. Suddenly a door opened and another heart fell in step with complete synchrony. Because only those who have felt a deep hurt can understand, just about everyone *can* understand. But not every heart-door stands open. And mine was not. So I played pretend and tried to keep the rest locked inside.

One night someone knocked on the door of my uncle's house. We opened the front door, and Julie screamed. The woman on the other side of the iron security screen door was my very own, in-the-flesh, Mom. Frantic hands reached through bars, afraid the dream might slip away into the night. Panic set in at the thought. Aunt Bonnie fumbled the keys into the door, surprised at our desperation to get through. For a few seconds we had slipped out of pretending.

Mom came all the way from Zambia to see us. For a few days we celebrated with her, staying in a nearby flat. I don't remember how long we were together. I only know it was too short.

Most of the time it was just easier to stay behind the veil. Easier to go numb and pretend to live and like another's reality. Play the chameleon. Blend in. I *pretended* I belonged, though I didn't feel it. But the inner chasm of grief and chaos never left.

It festered.

I know that now. I also know that more people are willing to cross over into another's grief than I ever thought. Not because they understand the ache of boarding school, but because grief itself is a common thread. Grief and loss are part of the human condition.

Instead of being a reason for separation, it becomes a way to stitch our heart to others.

Grief isn't culturally defined. It isn't confined by nationality or skin color or language. It's as human as the smile. To live veiled is as ridiculous and empty as apartheid. It only took me thirty years to figure that out. I thank God a few people made it through the veil of my childhood.

Academically I suffered. Math stopped making sense. Everything else felt irrelevant. It may have been the reflection of a young student struggling under the vagaries of different countries' educational systems. Most of it was the result of the fester.

I wouldn't learn how to be a student until much later.

28

Term Break

Ndola, 1984

I still remember the day.

Washing the van. Garden hose in hand. Barefoot as usual. Sudsy hands. Delicious sunshine.

A concrete water tower compensated for city water pumps that couldn't match the demand. Water pressure disappeared during the day, but our tank filled up at night. As a result, we had real live water spurting from the garden hose.

Dad stopped on his walk from house to office and asked if we might be interested in staying home and trying correspondence school instead of going back to South Africa.

I couldn't believe it.

The water kept flowing and bits of sunlight got stuck in the bubbles dripping from my hands. He might have said more. I don't remember. Time froze.

All I heard was 'stay home.'

In that moment, the entire weight of boarding school and going away and the creeping shadows of an encroaching term scattered as surely as cockroaches when the light comes on. It left me so certainly, I decided to put that part of my story away. There by the van with my bare feet and a lump in my throat I cut off the first chapters of my life and threw them out.

A little person in me had been holding his breath until that moment. He started to breathe and part of me came back to life.

What was presented as a casual question added color to my grey world. It is one of the most pivotal moments of my story.

This eleven-year-old was home for good.

Thus began the happy years.

If anyone asked, our standard response was, "Boarding school was a good experience." I maintained that opinion until my first child turned five. Only then did I come to pieces. Abruptly, I came to grips with the impact of boarding school on my young heart. And only then did the healing start.

29

1985

I had done so well in South Africa, it was determined I should do fifth grade again. My correspondence course arrived in the mail from Calvert School in Baltimore, Maryland, a place I had never been. The curriculum required I mail completed lessons and examinations to the Baltimore teachers. These were graded and returned. A 15,178 mile round-trip. Not exactly immediate feedback. Julie's lessons went to Nebraska.

The fat assignments manual outlined the daily drill. Math. Art History. English....

I sat at the desk in the living room, checking off the items in my book, doing as few of the math practice problems as possible. I actually enjoyed art history, embracing for the first time the creative genius of others. The sculptures and magnificent architectural masterpieces filled my head with a cultural influence far beyond the realm of my experience.

I started to learn about myself. Without the prospect of returning to a boarding-school, dreams started to formulate. Now that I was out of prison, the whole world lay before me.

My folks always said I should do whatever I wanted with my life. It was then, during my second round of fifth grade I decided I might want to be a writer.

Not that I liked reading, mind you.

Mom taught me that vocabulary can be delicious. She showed me that a word, well placed, is ever so satisfying. Mom labored with me over my essays, helping me pick 'just the right word.'

One of the first stories I wrote was about a boy who ran away from boarding school, escaping by hiding in the trees. I suppose it was mildly cathartic.

Though I wanted to be a writer, I also wanted to fly planes and build things. Within the next twenty years I fashioned my first boat from two plastic pickle barrels bolted together. Later, I managed a traditional Indian rickshaw built over the used, front axle and wheel assembly of a retired Amish buggy. Then came the mahogany expedition kayak, and the renovation of several early American homes with the help of Keith Newswanger who unstintingly taught me just about everything I know related to construction.

But in the fifth grade, I didn't know any of that. I created with Lego and tinkered in Dad's shop. I elbowed up next to him while he made a ukulele from an old oil tin. Not exactly luthier-quality, and I found the *making* more fun than the playing.

I upgraded to Dad's guitar. Julie and I took lessons from Carolyn Belton down the street. Playing came easily, and soon I was joining my friends in jam sessions, learning anything I could.

Being home was so much better! We took every meal with Mom and Dad. Mom helped us 'build character' with various household chores. Unlike many white families around us, we didn't employ house help. The whole concept of house-help to many western minds is deeply connected with racial bigotry. The difference is that in America, people have grocery stores, washing machines, dryers and dishwashers. It's just a different kind of house help. Someone—probably grossly underpaid—had to grow those vegetables or build that machine in China. The distance from underpaid and under-appreciated laborer to the American citizen is greater, but it's still there, buried in technology that's taken for granted.

But we did our own work because we liked the privacy of being on our own.

30

Gardenia trees bloomed around the garden. Avocado, banana and guava provided shade, and a granadilla (or passion fruit) vine hung by the walk.

Mom occasionally made it into juice if we hadn't already broken open the purple, shriveling pods and sucked out their tart bellies-full of seedy pulp. The pulp, though tasty, shares a consistency similar to snot.

Avocados dropped from a huge tree just out the back door. If we grabbed them before the dogs, they became part of a favorite breakfast. Avocado on toast with Marmite can mend a broken heart or still raging waters. And a thin film of marmite over fried rice cakes made from yesterday's leftover rice is as close to high culture as I care to be, thank you.

To have both at the same meal is the Kiss of Heaven.

A guava tree goes to fruit with gusto and the hard round nobs swell to the size of racket balls. As a guava grows, the dark green skin softens to chartreuse and ever so slowly turns yellow. That place somewhere between green and yellow is the perfect guava. Skin mildly tart, sweet flesh with a seedy center the texture of firm custard.

To pick a guava one must walk the narrow line between perfection and strange encounters as human's aren't the only hungry creatures.

Fruit bats managed to steal their share, leaving the half-eaten remnants of their gluttony littered beneath the tree to attract flies. Worse, was a species of white worm that frequented the inside of a ripening guava and offered a similar textural experience to the aforementioned custard. The worms probably inhabited the fruit while it was green, but were too small to see. They didn't bother me.

A sweeter, softer guava can be had, but at a price. Those were best eaten with eyes shut, or wide open and very slowly.

Even though our low tree offered plenty of fruit within easy reach, I regularly climbed the slippery bark in a quest for a better guava, often eating half a fruit before discovering the worm and realizing I had come late to the meal. I dropped the half-eaten guava and the half-eaten worm to rot with the bat's leftovers in the grass below.

Mom knew how to make the most of a guava. One of her favorite treats was guava in Bird's custard. Julie and I brought in the bounty, so she could work her magic. In a land where the number of ingredients for a culinary presentation were limited, guavas— occupied or not—were on the menu.

I asked Mom about the worms. She batted her eye lashes conspiratorially and smiled, "Extra protein."

Besides, the addition of custard made the worms almost impossible to see. Good thing, too. She usually served it for guests.

Julie and I, full to the brim with *knowing*, brought out bowls of custard to exclamations of happy ebullience from our guests. Our secret. Mom smiled at us across the table as she dipped in her spoon.

In our family, we ate *everything* on our plate. She must have worked a kind of magic, because for all that, it *was* delicious.

31

During our years in Zambia, one of the more unique pets we acquired was Puzzle, so named after the ass in C.S. Lewis's Chronicles of Narnia. Puzzle was an African Grey Parrot. A distinctly intelligent breed, the African Grey has held world records for the largest number of memorized phrases and songs.

The only problem with our Puzzle was that he said not a word. Not even one "hello."

He clicked and hooted like an owl, but nothing more. Turning his head to the side, Puzzle stared us down with a single yellow eye.

I don't know how we acquired him, but he romped happily about the cage which sat by the dining room window with a view of the guava tree. We clipped his wing feathers as insurance against him making for the deep, dark Congo Rain Forest up north from whence he came. Every now and again, we opened the cage door and Puzzle climbed around the outside of his domain, pretending to take off, but never releasing his grip on the cage. His flapping made a terrific noise and stirred up every loose feather preened from his silky grey coat. The mess ascended like a miniature flurry and settled again when he was done showing off.

Once, deciding he needed fresh air and exercise, we let Puzzle hike around the guava tree. That day, as I labored over math at the desk in my bedroom, I heard a man shouting in the back yard. Coming out of my daze, I raced out the back door. Bimbo, our German Shepherd and Cindy, the Doberman, stood on point at the base of the guava tree. Puzzle had slipped and landed squarely in the lion's den.

119

A lesser bird would have been quick food. Our dogs had a reputation to uphold.

I've never heard a parrot yell gibberish with such complete confidence. He sounded like a man shouting down someone who'd cut him off on the interstate. Only it made no sense. I pushed past the be-hackled dogs and put my arm down for the bird. He made haste to high ground. I held him above the threatening dogs and retreated into the safety of the indoors.

It's a jungle out there.

Bimbo and Cindy returned to loll in the shade.

Lolling, however, was something at which Bimbo did not excel. The dog never lay down for more than a few seconds. Bimbo's internal buzzer went off and he'd be up and pacing, panting furiously all the time. After a few circles, he made another attempt at lolling, but it was always the same. Perhaps the gene pool for breeding German Shepherds had run shallow in Zambia. Bimbo drove Dad to distraction.

Even though the dogs lived outside, squadrons of fleas assembled in dry season and soon made a run on the house, undergirded by the tune from that old Salvation Army hymn, *"Oh, when the Saints, go marching in."*

We'd notice specks of dirt popping up around our ankles in the living room, like micro-sized black popcorn.

The spots landed and bit. Mom declared war.

Although we lived in town, it was still Africa and creepy crawlies were ubiquitous.

Mom seldom fussed about critters. She'd managed the bush and the mortuary, remember. But fleas made her bare arms. Or is that bear arms?

Once the fleas invaded, Dad procured the requisite pesticide bombs, covered our food, set them off throughout the house, and we'd go away for a while.

When we returned, carnage was everywhere.

What a happy, powerful feeling.

The other creature that pushed Mom to violent means were ants. The particular ants Mom despised were not the kind one might expect. Zambia does, after all, boast some fantastic varieties. There's the Zozo, a local name for an ant that is probably known elsewhere as the Matabele ant. Huge monsters, these. Termite hunters, I think. You could actually hear these suckers walk! Nor was it the red ants (army ants) who traveled in highly organized flanks with the largest, baddest sentries posted on the edges.

What salted Mom were sugar ants. These fellows are a fraction of the size of Zambia's more prominent species. But they were counter-top food thieves, and for this reason Mom hated them.

Many times I walked into the kitchen to find her beating a loaf of fresh banana bread on the counter. She wasn't trying to beat the ants to death, per se, just shake them out.

Death came later.

"Oh, fooey," she spat.

I'm not kidding. *Fooey*. Although Mom never said it then, what she *wanted* to say, was, "This is my bread, dammit. Give it back." We were seven thousand miles away from the land of Tasty Cakes.

The eleventh ant commandment. "Thou shalt not stand between a missionary woman and her made-from-scratch banana bread."

I didn't know until much later that although Mom frequently cooked up the miraculous (liver excepted), she never liked baking.

Sugar ants are bitter. And as she was *not* going to share her bread with them, she shook the devil out of it. Still, they burrow. A loaf of banana bread made from sickly-sweet and black, over-ripe bananas was like edible earth. They couldn't resist.

War was declared and mom started bludgeoning them to death right there on the counter. I cannot now remember if she used the banana bread or a knobkerrie to mete out the fatal blows.

32

Zambia had a reasonably impressive collection of ugly spiders. Not many were poisonous, but in my experience, the heebie-jeebie factor of a spider has nothing to do with its *actual* danger.

Wall spiders weren't so bad so long as they stayed in their place. These critters, though several inches from toe to toe, run pancake-flat across the wall, slipping perfectly under the next picture frame. Mom didn't seem to mind these either.

Maybe she figured they were on her team. Both Mom and the wall spiders wanted mosquitoes dead. A few extra spiders beat a round of malaria, hands-down. Mom would call out, "Hi, bu-uddy" whenever a particularly energetic one scampered from picture frame to picture frame. Though they never reached celebrity status for their mosquito culls, even I managed an uneasy peace with this version of the arachnid family.

Until they got on the floor. Don't ask why, but if you take a perfectly flat black and brown-striped wall spider and put him on the floor he turns into a NOT FLAT flurry of legs and panic and get-me-back-to-the-wall. Their legs hump up in great arches and they stagger along in a rage of insecurity.

Another time I rode on the back of Dad's motorcycle as he explored a bush track off the main road. It was just like Dad to turn off the main road in favor of the bush. I smiled. The adventure had begun. Quite suddenly the bike came to an abrupt halt, mashing my face up inside my helmet against Dad's back. He had stumbled into the web of an *arachnida jurassica*. His landing gear came out, and he started the ungainly back pedal routine. I was forced back on the seat and the bike tottered. The spider he'd knocked down from the web was doing the Frankenstein-walk toward the rear tire. Dad's foot came down and the spider popped with the sound of a small melon.

Why is it that the spirit of a murdered spider has to crawl across the back of your neck before it crosses the river Styx?

If you like spiders, then you have no idea what I'm talking about. I'll get to you with the snake stories further on.

Spiders are attracted to me in the same way cats are attracted to people who hate them.

Later in life I was back in Zambia after Doe and I got married and made three kids. The spiders kept coming.

Lusaka has these nasty, see-throughish suckers known locally as 'posties.' They burst from beneath a chair, blatantly disregarding bare toes, rushing who-knows-where, dragging extra sets of legs behind them. Really. That's what it looks like. Of course, they're purported to be poisonous, which doesn't do much to improve the general bonhomie.

Doe and I moved into the bush of Zambia's Western Province. This part of the country shares the same geology as the Kalahari Desert but with significantly more rainfall. The Zambezian miombo woodlands stand over sandy soils. Adequate rainfall birthed thick vegetation and the grass grew green along the river plains. The posties were just a warm up.

We moved to a cottage on the edge of the Luampa River plain.

Not long after we settled in, the first spider assassin came after me. He waited by the bed. My side of the bed, mind you. He was looking for me. Roughly the size of a miniature tumble weed, crouched and ready to strike.

But I've been at this game for a while. My spider sense started tingling and I saw him before he saw me. I slipped from the room and returned with a can of "Doom," Zambia's kill-'em-all spray. My spurs scraped the floor. A finger twitched over the trigger. I heard a wild-west whistle followed by the hustle of Spanish guitars. I think we might have circled each other.

Then I let him have it.

The cloud of death-spray overwhelmed the creature. He curled up on himself like a crumpled ball of yarn. The hiss of Doom continued until the bottle started to spit and Doe coughed through the cloud on her side of the bed. It looked like I'd been playing with a fog machine.

Spider-zero. Dwight-one. So what if it took the whole can?

I didn't clean him up. Didn't want to touch him.

I took off my spurs and crawled into bed, brushing the spider spirit from the back of my neck a few times before tucking in the mosquito net.

I fell asleep wondering why spiders never bothered my wife, but content in the knowledge that I'd done my part to make the world a better place.

The next morning, I woke under the happy spell of the Cape Turtle Dove and yanked out the net to let my feet down. The toes curled before they hit the ground, remembering the creepy carcass I'd have to haul away. Where was my shovel?

Only one problem.

The spider was gone.

On instant replay, I imagined him unfurling his legs like a wet flag stretching out in a cold wind and saw him stagger off.

Ever have the feeling that something is after you?

Some months afterward, I walked to the kitchen, bound for the gas stove. The electricity hadn't come on yet and besides, there is only one way to make a decent pot of tea.

It is my firm opinion that a man shouldn't have to make serious decisions or fight any battles until after he's imbibed the requisite amount of hot tea. With milk and sugar. It's the African way.

I stopped cold. Another assassin blocked my way to the sink. This guy was the most impressive spider I'd ever seen. I had to give him that. But something was off. I leaned in a bit to count his legs. Ten. I worked counter-clock wise. Still ten.

And on top of that, he had a handsome pair of saber-studded scimitars for teeth.

I know something about spiders, as one does growing up in Africa. A spider, by definition, is an eight-legged ugly.

Insects have six, spiders eight. What do you call the ten-legged version?

Demonic.

What was worse, this guy's hair looked like a balding man's greasy comb-over.

There was only one thing to do. I removed my Jesus sandal and raised it over my head, ready to strike. After all, what would Jesus do?

Send it straight to hell.

But before I became the instrument of God's judgment, the demon-spider rose up on its back four legs and pawed the air.

I kid you not. It reared like a mythical centaur brandishing his sword before battle and gnashed its teeth.

Sometime later, I stumbled across an article of a similar species in a National Geographic magazine. Apparently, they're known as wind scorpions. The extra set of 'legs' (pedipalps) are actually sensory organs. According to the article, this spider has (relative to their size) the strongest bite in the animal kingdom and has been known to catch and eat lizards and birds.

Birds are warm blooded. I'm warm blooded.

The demon was after me; I felt it.

In fact, the spirits of his deceased relatives were already playing hokey pokey on my neck.

The demon met the Jesus sandal.

Demon's always lose with these odds. I had to dial back the religious zeal because my efforts rendered him limbless and small, significantly diminishing his value for show and tell.

Demon spider – zero. Jesus sandal – one.

Why is it a dead spider always seems eight times smaller when it's dead? I know why. The spider spirit leaks out and crawls over the assailant. They are actually stinging and biting, but they can't break through the veil of the other world to have any real effect.

Word got out, I suppose. A frontal assault wasn't going to work. Assassin three made a plan.

Most spider species take abseiling lessons before they enter pre-school. This fellow practiced without ropes.

It's not like I have a vindictive streak. I was minding my own business. I'm not after every spider in the world. I just don't go for the kind who lie in wait.

I opened the door to our shed and stepped inside. Assassin three dropped from above. I felt him brush past my cheek and neck before landing by my feet. No spider spirits this time. It was the real-deal, hairy spider feet on my neck.

Doe was inside the house visiting with a friend. They heard a woman's blood curdling scream from the back yard.

"What's that noise?" asked her friend.

"Oh. That's Dwight," Doe replied, blandly. "He must have seen a spider."

Now officially, Zambia doesn't have tarantulas. But the Western Province grows hideous monsters which, for all intents and purposes, *are* tarantulas. I think they're officially the baboon spider, likely named because they are hairy and dog-butt ugly. Their bite is poisonous enough to make one vomit, feel weak and dizzy.

A couple of kids showed me one of these nasties in an empty peanut-butter jar. The creature walked it around like a hamster in a plastic ball.

Have you ever heard a dog trying to accelerate on a tile floor? That's (almost) what this spider sounded like as it scampered away, my boots in hot pursuit.

Jesus was not involved and the spider got away. It didn't bite me, yet I felt, nonetheless nauseated, weak and dizzy.

Spiders rank up there with life's greatest mysteries. What is the meaning of life? Why do good people suffer? Why are there spiders?

33

While Zambia can boast the fairest weather on the planet, humans aren't the only creatures who have noticed. Snakes also take to the fine climate and thrive there.

Somewhere along the way we heard that 98% of Zambian snakes were deadly. The two innocuous ones being the blind snake and the file snake.

Poppycock, you say? Fine. When it comes time to play nicey-nice with a snake, I'll let you go first. We lived under the assumption that (almost) every snake was poisonous.

Some people, warped by hippie ideology, who live in the comfort of an almost snake-less world, preach a St. Francis-friendly, save-the-snakes message. My parents took a hard line. The only good snake was a dead snake. A far safer modus operandi.

At boarding school, we had a class on Zambia's more stunning species. On at least one occasion the teacher pointed out the window to reference a textbook example sunning himself in a tree. (Who needs books?) Boomslangs, puff adders, gaboon vipers, black mambas and spitting cobras framed my basic understanding of those cursed in Eden. Snakes could kill. Some quite effectively.

Considering the fact that people actually had been killed by snakes in the areas where we lived, dire warnings fell on fertile soil. We walked with our eyes on the path.

As did everyone.

The gaboon viper was a personal favorite, if favorite is the correct word here. The toxic capacity of this particular specimen might have something to do with the sheer volume of venom it can discharge in a moment of rage. According to my boarding school teacher, this creature was blessed with *two* separate poisons. One traveled through the bloodstream causing cardiac arrest. The second made a victim bleed out, internally or elsewhere. How pleasant. This viper 'jumped' to strike, landing its venom closer to the main breaker.

A gaboon viper's pattern is quite fetching. The perfect combination of leafy blotches made the creature ridiculously hard to spot. As a consequence, animals as sensorily adroit as the lion might inadvertently tread upon one of these. When the lion treads upon the viper, the lion ends up dead.

While the threat of snakes didn't slow us down much, we lived aware that we shared the 'neighborhood,' as it were.

While camping near the Kabompo River, Julie lolled on a blanket in the shade reading. I threatened birds with a BB gun. I plinked away into the tree overhead. After a while, we heard a rustling and a thump, not far from the blanket. Julie glanced up from her book just in time to stare eye-to-eye with a displaced boomslang.

With black eyes oversized for its face, the boomslang doesn't exactly cut as intimidating a figure as the more heavily patterned species. Black highlights over an emerald green might be pretty on a dress, but not so on a snake. Boom means 'tree' in Afrikaans or Dutch. In keeping with its name, this particular slang likes to hang out in trees where adults can grow to a comfortable six feet in length. It is deadly. A bite from a boomslang causes hemorrhage. While antivenom *might* have been available in a fridge somewhere in the country, the likelihood of actually *finding* treatment in real time was thin. If a person failed to get treatment soon enough, a complete blood transfusion was sometimes a last recourse. But blood banks needed to be kept cold, which required refrigeration. Not gonna happen in the bush. I needn't mention the concomitant risks associated with blood transfusions in Africa at that time.

Getting help in the bush is trickier than dialing 911. Emergencies of this magnitude usually set in motion a complicated chain of events.

The news would be relayed at the next radio transmission to Mukinge hospital. Depending on the situation (and the weather), a mission plane might be scrambled to the closest bush airstrip. But with no runway lights, the plane had to make the destination before sunset or wait until the next morning. In the meantime, those on the ground had to shoo away animals grazing on the field as propellers offer an ineffectual method of butchering.

If no bush plane could make the emergency run, the snake victim might have to be ferried by vehicle four bumpy hours to a hospital that may not be able to help them anyway. In especially dire circumstances, a family might spring for an emergency medical airlift to South Africa where they had the best medical facilities on the continent. But the medi-vac companies (operating out of Johannesburg) couldn't make a bush landing either, so the patient still had to be ferried to the international airport in Lusaka.

The best option was not to let them bite you in the first place.

Julie and the boomslang stared at each other for one of those eternal seconds experienced in horror movies. Then she barrel-rolled in the opposite direction, and we both switched into high-speed evasive maneuvers.

Julie blubbered for a while after that. Considering she had just stared death in the face, I didn't much blame her.

I suffered only from a stubbed toe which had done me the disservice of hanging low when I made good my escape.

Dad beat round the grass for a while with a **grass slasher**, but the slang had long since made good his escape. Mom tried to comfort Julie with the standard line, "Snakes are more afraid of you than you are of them."

In Julie's case, right then, I sincerely doubted that.

A notable exception to the 'more afraid of you' line was the black mamba. The black mamba has earned the distinction of being Africa's deadliest snake. This is something of a misnomer, because he is endowed with only one poison whereas his richer brother, the gaboon viper, has two. Still, the mamba rightly holds the land title for dangerous snake because what he lacks in fetching patterns and lengthy fangs, he makes up for with aggressive nastiness.

The black mamba is a snake that lives perpetually resentful of his fallen state. The least slight or imposition will throw a mamba into a dyspeptic rage. I should mention, the black mamba isn't actually black. He sports more of a silver-grey finish. The name is derived from the color inside its mouth.

Not a detail I care to field check.

An irritated mamba can pull one third of his body off the ground. That means a full-grown, fourteen-foot snake can strike an almost five-foot pose, staring a victim in the eye just before he sends them into the afterlife. This is all rather impressive on paper, but add the fact that a mamba is one of the fastest snakes on the planet, and one begins to see the perils of ticking-off the wrong snake. Odds lean decidedly in their favor. It's just not fair.

I've heard of men who drove over a black mamba and it chased them down. One man managed to get the tires on the snakes' body and watched with morbid fascination as it struck repeatedly against the windscreen of the Land Rover, smearing its vile poison across the glass in a vain attempt to mete out revenge.

Another man told the story of an ill-fated herd of cattle that trespassed on a mamba's personal space. The writhing serpent struck out at the panicked herd. In a matter of minutes, fifteen cattle lay dead.

Impressive stuff. But you know how stories go. And grow.

Grandpa Kopp once went out to tend to a cobra holed up between fifty-five gallon drums behind his house. (Cobra's make a rather impressive hissing noise when they're upset.) While Grandpa and a few other men were in the process of trying to chase the snake out of hiding, the creature peeked out and unloaded a mouthful of venom into Grandpa's eyes.

Venom from the black-necked or Zebra-striped spitting cobra can cause blindness. The pain was excruciating and the boys (my Dad and his brothers) escorted Grandpa back to the house while others went after the snake. The poison needs to be rinsed immediately and milk is recommended to neutralize the toxins. In dire situations where there was no alternative, some have urinated into the victim's eye. That tends to be a bit tricky and kind of hard to explain afterwards. Thankfully water was handy. Finding milk, on the other hand, was more problematic.

A batch of powdered milk was hurriedly mixed. Grandpa was restrained and they pried his eyelids open to administer the milk. The milk (even powdered) did the trick and Grandpa suffered no ill effects.

The blokes outside conquered the snake, which ended up being a mere six foot long. They subsequently identified it as a spitting cobra. No kidding. That's like waiting for someone to die before declaring the snake as 'deadly.'

We shared space with these wonderful creatures. So when Roger and Barbara Kemp and kids came to Chizela, it was only fitting that we have a snake event in honor of their visit.

One (large, black and probably deadly) had been spotted in a tree. Martin and Judith Kemp were longtime friends, roughly the same age as Julie and I. Together we joined in the fun of filling the creature with BB's while a Kaonde man with remarkable aim hammered the snake with rocks. Still the creature clung to its branch. (Snakes, incidentally, die slowly.) The battle was set. We weren't backing down. It was him or us.

133

Considering it was up a tree, and we were a safe distance away, this seemed like a reasonable proposition.

The day wore on. Evening approached. And the snake continued to writhe, looping itself back onto the tree every time a rock hit the mark.

At last it fell. Our sense of security vanished now that we were on the same floor. But the villagers finished him off, and we dragged the creature back home as the tip of its tail curled around our fingers. We counted the BB holes. 26!

With darkness comes a certain shift in perspective. A snake killed in daylight, stalks when the lights go out.

I closed my eyes and snakes hung down from the bunk overhead. I opened my eyes.

Time for reinforcements.

"Dad!"

My parents remember that night as a sleepless event. Each parent paired off with a child, attempting with empty words to still the horrors of imaginations fed by memories of a cursed, slithering snake that refused to die.

A nearby parent has an amazing ability to fend off a case of night-time horrors.

Good times.

David Pedersen was a buddy of mine in Ndola who mastered the art of skinning a snake. However, a snake that is bludgeoned to death by an eager almost-victim didn't make for a great specimen. A snake whose head is blown off with a shotgun offers a similarly unattractive sheath. After all, the head skin (though difficult to manage) is an important part of the whole.

Once, David and I took a snake-hunting expedition into the bush near his home. We took forked sticks with us so we could give it the business. Eventually, we came upon a sleeping baby puff adder. The neonates are born venomous, and it wasn't hard to take the fingerling seriously. The puff adder is reported to be the cause of almost 35,000 deaths per year on the continent. The adder's habitat extends over most of Africa and touches on the Arabian Peninsula. Because of its broad range and the fact that it is reasonably bad tempered, the puff adder boasts the greatest number of human kills. Whereas a victim of the black mamba will be dead in twenty minutes, a puff adder bite starts a twenty-five hour ordeal. This usually involves necrotic tissue, skin sloughing off and possible limb amputation.

Then you die.

David told me the best way to kill a snake was with a piece of flexible hose. A section of garden hose offers several advantages over a stick. Whereas a solid stick will hit the ground in only one place, a garden hose provides a greater range of contact. Because killing a snake is a him-or-me proposition, any advantage is welcome. Adrenaline hasn't necessarily been connected with improved aim, and the prospect of flailing away at a moving rope of death without making contact is unsavory. I believe in the hose-pipe method.

Word was out around David's home about his interest in snakes. Villagers brought in snakes they killed for him to skin. He was particularly excited when a woman brought him a heavy, moving, burlap bag holding an adder or viper.

Not wanting to damage what might be a perfect and undamaged skin, David decided to drown the snake and so placed the snake— burlap-bag-and-all—into a watering trough for the night.

In the morning, he retrieved the snake and turned it belly up on the skinning board. Skinning a snake is nothing like peeling a carrot. The patterned skin on a snake does not extend to the belly scales, so the snake must be un-zipped down the front. David pressed his blade into the skin under the jaw, cutting through the scales in a line down the center. Once the skin is flayed open, the unattractive belly skin serves as a border that can be nailed to the drying board. David put down his knife and began to peel the skin back. When he got past the first lung to the heart, he noticed something wasn't right. It was still beating.

It went back into the water for a while. As mentioned, snakes die slowly.

So do snake stories.

34

Ndola 1986

When I was twelve years old, I joined Dad at the local squash club five days a week. We'd leave the house early and meet our friends at the club when it opened.

The squash club became a forum for interacting. After a game, I'd sit, red-faced, above the court and watch Dad and Uncle Harald Holmgren. Squash, for the uninitiated, is like racquet-ball except the ball doesn't bounce. It is played in a similar room, but with upper boundaries marked in red on four walls.

Most of my athletic endeavors were not team oriented. Kayaking, windsurfing, running and squash.

But I had friends in Ndola like I'd never had before because our friendships weren't confined to the parameters of a school term. These lasted longer and grew stronger. Aaron and Sam Salisbury and a few others became an integral part of my Africa story. They were the best kind of friends.

The Salisbury boys had finished up at Sakeji after grade seven and moved into the world of home-school. They also lived in Ndola, a few blocks and a short bicycle ride away. You could always tell which white guys grew up in Zambia because when they spoke a Bantu language, it sounded just right. Uncle Dave, their Dad, was one of these.

At least, that's how I remember it.

Their family had a certain playfulness about them. They liked music, turbo charged pick-up trucks, and crocodile hunting from jet boats. I learned that jet boats were a big thing in Kiwi land. Aaron is the only person I know who survived a crocodile bite. His injuries were minor. The croc was only twelve inches long.

Sam and Aaron were older than me, but they embraced my friendship enthusiastically. Both played rugby. I think one of their uncles played for the New Zealand All Blacks—a team name, not a racial reference and arguably the world's most well-known rugby team. They inherited a certain size and strength of frame which I had not, owing to the aforementioned powdered milk. Still, I was invited to practice with the team.

Rarely, me-thinks, has so motley a band of misfits gathered for training. Representing various ages and colors, these were the men with enough courage to put down their beers long enough to sweat and swear through the grueling session meted out by the coach. I joined them for practice but was too young to play.

After practice, the players gathered at the club bar where I joined them to drink bitter tonic water, eat biltong and listen to lies.

I loved watching the games. I had a barely functional understanding of the rules: Run the ball that way. Don't get caught. Stay away from the fat ones. Don't get stuck underneath.

Sam was amazing to watch. He was fast and strong, with fire in his eye and a permanent grin that made you feel the fun he was having.

Aaron and Sam, two and four years older respectively, were like big brothers. And they hadn't been assigned the job by the dorm mum. Their consideration might have had something to do with the fact that I had a pretty, older sister who hung out with us. Regardless, it was the first time beyond the Monkey Gang, where I felt belonging outside of my home.

A memoir isn't supposed to be a place for sappy gratitude. But the friendship they poured into me filled empty places I didn't know existed. I only wish that every man might be lucky enough to have a few friends like this along the journey of his life.

Dave Salisbury, their dad, attended Sakeji around the time my dad was there. Though they hailed from New Zealand, they also lived out their lives in Zambia and drew me into adventure. David Pederson (a Dane) joined the fun. As did Ben Byrd and others. We hung out together because we understood each other in a way only those caught between worlds can. The world of the 'other' and the world of Africa's present. We lived together on the moon.

In an effort to get in touch with our warrior hearts, we crowded into Dad's workshop and hammered pipes into swords. We fashioned spears and transformed nails and cotton balls into blow-gun darts. I found an enormous bush knife among Dad's gear. It had been used to butcher elephants and hippos and who knew what else. He gave it to me, and in so doing called me into manhood.

This prized possession became the foundation for a collection of fixed blade knives that grew over the years to include a Maori skinning knife from New Zealand, handmade village knives sharpened on stones, and a Nepalese Gurkha Kukri purchased by way of *Ye Olde Curiosity Shop* along the Seattle waterfront.

The avocado tree suffered innumerable wounds as I practiced with my tactical throwing knife. The banana grove became a combat zone. Real men, after all, can topple a banana tree with one slice of the blade. The trunk, nature's version of cardboard rolled into a tight cylinder, provided the perfect target.

35

Bananas are the most curious of trees. The dense leafy stem bleeds clear, sticky sap which I'm told will keep you alive if you're dying of thirst. In truth, you might have to be near death to want to drink it.

Our banana grove surrounded a trash pit. The pit was our personal landfill. Everyone had one. Most were roughly six by six by six foot cubes cut neatly into the clay ground. In the absence of adequate trash collection, all waste made it into the pit which was periodically burned. Living banana trees have such a high water content that they don't easily catch on fire.

One burn day I followed Dad out and watched him dump Diesel fuel and petrol (gasoline) on the rubbish.

"Can I light it?" A standard almost-man question.

Dad paused. Considering. He wasn't averse to sharing the fun. "You'd better let me do it."

Good move.

I stood back. Thirty feet. Dad lit a roll of burning newspaper, dropped it into the hole and turned away.

Fumes from fuel, I learned, can be quite explosive.

The match ignited a flame that shot thirty feet into the air, creating a concussive blast that launched Dad out of the banana grove. He actually flew—Superman style. He landed—not Superman style—

several meters away. The eruption of fire resolved into a ball of greasy black smoke overhead. Banana leaves curled over angry tongues of fire fed by the detritus of our lives.

Mom came running from the house, probably expecting guerrilla activity.

The blast was loud enough to have been mistaken as an act of terror. Explosions of that size have plunged similarly insecure countries into a state of war. But military choppers didn't fly over and the police didn't show. No surprise there.

Dad, however, hadn't fared so well. The fire badly burned his forearm and shortened his eyelashes to a row of black pearls on short stems.

I don't ever remember Mom or Dad yelling at each other. It just wasn't their way. When Dad was in trouble, he became "Timothy John." They managed to work side by side in cross-cultural situations and veritable war zones that would have driven most people to sniveling heaps, fetal-bound in some corner. There is conflict in every marriage, but they always came out *together* on the other side. Their love for God and each other carried them through quite a bit.

What was a small, back-yard explosion? The son (me) was alive. The dogs might have experienced some residual psychological trauma, but with Bimbo that was hard to tell. The banana leaves still curling under the flames outside would be quickly replaced.

I watched, eyes wide while Mom bandaged and nursed and "Timothy John-ed" him.

Dad submitted to Mom's remonstrations, playing the role of the properly-penitent. After all, he was in trouble *because* she loved him. But there remained an unmistakable twinkle in his eyes. Though burnt and a little embarrassed, Dad had made a bomb and thoroughly enjoyed seeing it go boom.

Dad loved adventure. Maybe that's why he liked living in the bush.

Maybe he liked getting stuck, too.

36

Having a bike to ride out the front gate was, for me, like owning my first car. I spent hours with friends spinning around Ndola, finding ramps when we could, building them when we couldn't. The bicycle years fed a new-found independence. For the first time, I felt anchored at home yet was free to launch out. My folks didn't mind me riding around town. I didn't feel conspicuously white, though we most certainly were. Everywhere we went we drew stares. I suppose I just got used to it. It had always been that way.

One day we built a ramp in Sam and Aaron's back yard. It was a short hard pile with a deliciously steep ascent. We raked together a pile of leaves and set it on fire.

I lined up, hit the ramp, and sailed into the air over the flames. For a fleeting instant I felt like Elliot, only ET wasn't in my basket and midflight I realized something was going terribly wrong. My front wheel continued to lift and the bike landed in a near vertical situation. The force of impact propelled me unceremoniously to the ground, feet and arms still in the drive position. Without my landing gear underneath, my tailbone hammered hard into the ground.

I spent a while down there, writhing, gasping and dragging my bottom across the dirt like a dog with worms.

My friends cried their eyes out. Aaron and Sam were not ones to pass on such a brilliant occasion for a laugh.

Public misadventures are worse with white skin in a black world as it makes disappearing into the woodwork a bit harder.

Another day, I was sailing down the hill on my way to link up with the Salisbury boys, listening to the knobby tires speeding up on the barely-tarred road. The abrupt T-junction at the bottom of the hill didn't bother me. Wouldn't have bothered me.

But my chain came off. It was the days of pedal brakes. No chain equals no brakes.

I hate it when that happens.

That was when I noticed the number of people walking along the road who would now bear witness to the white-boy projectile I was about to become.

I needed an immediate plan. The rubber tires hummed louder, spinning closer to the launch site. I made my move. Lifting my right foot off the pedal, I swung my leg over the seat and stood on the remaining pedal, working out the next step of the maneuver. Pulling my right foot forward, I stepped down in front of my left pedal. A shoe-on-earth should work like a brake, right?

Wrong.

It worked like a pole vault. The whole business (including me) shot into the air without ceremony. I tumbled ass-over-lid down the center of the road while a throng of horrified women watched the white-silver-rubber flash of my chaotic gymnastic gone wrong. I created an open-air smoothie blender—the bike-as-blade lashing out at the white-boy banana.

When the mess that was me finally untangled itself, the whole world of watchers had come to a standstill. Women—statue like—studied the wreckage with towering loads balanced on their heads.

Pain seared into my leg where blood provided color contrast. But my want-to-blend-in pride forced an ambivalent shrug. I didn't wait for anyone to assist me.

Nothing to see here.

I fixed the chain and limp-rode the rest of the way to the house where Sam and Aaron were waiting. The home of a mechanic-friend of theirs.

Aaron shinnied up a pomegranate tree and soon we were happily chewing and spewing seeds. I pushed back the blistering pain in my leg and salvaged what I could from the incident into a healing narrative.

After all, stories make the world go round.

37

If memory serves, it was the Salisbury's mechanic-friend who asked them to deliver a BMW sedan from South Africa, and I wanted to see the bimmer.

Sam and his dad had brought it through Botswana where the roads were good and the tar was fast. After all, a BMW needs elbow room and Botswana was just the ticket. But their trip had a bit of a hiccough. Some manner of antelope decided to leap across the road as they passed. The creature smashed the front windscreen (windshield), passing completely through the sedan's interior and out the back window without leaving a single scratch on bonnet or boot *(hood or trunk)*. However, the animal's sharp horn tore clean through the muscle of Sam's shoulder, leaving a bloody mess. In the split second before impact, Sam dodged half a tick to the side. Uncle Dave wasn't so fortunate and took it full in the face.

They stopped and curious black faces materialized from the bush to surround the car. But when the pedestrians saw dead (free) meat lying on the road behind them, most of the help disappeared. I don't know where they went to get patched up, but Sam had an impressive track of black stitches across his arm. It looked like he had been in a blade fight with Rambo.

They drove the rest of the way home with rugby socks wrapped around their faces to protect them from the bugs who, in the absence of a windscreen, committed hari-kari on their faces.

I saw Uncle Dave soon after. To say his head wasn't right for a while doesn't sound nice. But his head wasn't right for a while after that. The pain must have been extraordinary.

It is a miracle he wasn't killed. The seat's head rest kept his neck from breaking. Uncle Dave came around though, and was soon enough back to his gregarious, energetic self.

38

Worlds run parallel. It only feels awkward when one has to be part of both.

Sometime after Julie and I started correspondence school, we got a television. The Zambian National Broadcasting Corporation started their single channel daily broadcast at noon. The colored bars on the screen flicked to a recording of the national anthem.

"Stand and sing of Zambia, proud and free."

Evening shows included re-runs of American programs with kisses edited out for the sake of decency. With the kiss-cut, amorous actors hit an invisible force field and bounced away from each other.

Somewhere in there, I watched in horror as the Space Shuttle Challenger broke apart after takeoff. Only we watched it a little later than the rest of the world. It was the first time I had actually watched real people die. My keyhole got bigger.

But the channel also carried Magnum P.I. and The A-Team. Go figure.

I entered another world of contrasts. Inside was a private investigator in a red Ferrari and a group of crazy Americans who loved it "when a plan comes together."

Outside, barefoot kids sucked mango seeds and teased the dogs. Outside the general populace struggled to make ends meet in a city where bread lines and food shortages were commonplace.

After securing their independence from Britain in 1964, Dr. David Kenneth Kaunda was elected president. He eventually elbowed any opposition out of the way and set himself up as president for life.

He dressed in a tidy safari suit with a kisapi (traditional African cloth) sometimes draped about his shoulders and always carried a white handkerchief. The white hanky was the talisman of his rule. People whispered that it gave him power over the people. At any rate, his magic must have been stronger than Mushala's leopard skin, because in 1982 Kaunda's troops finally killed the rebel.

When a man-eating lion is killed, the villagers line up and stab the creature with their spears to claim a victory. It may have also been a way of signifying their disgust and, perhaps, because it was fun.

After Mushala was shot, the soldiers commenced a similar ritual and had to be restrained so the body wasn't mutilated beyond recognition.

The country might have done worse than Kaunda. If a man is going to function as a dictator, he might as well be a reasonably decent fellow. Kaunda, like most African national leaders at the time, was said to have a few skeletons in his closet, but his rule was generally considered less onerous than the likes of Mobutu Sese Seko of Zaire. Some even called Kaunda the Gandhi of Africa.

On the eve of Zambian Independence from England in 1964, Kaunda began the process of acquiring equity holdings in several foreign-owned interests, including the copper mines operated by the Anglo American Corporation and the Rhodesian Selection Trust.

But due to a spike in oil prices combined with the concurrent gross devaluation of copper on international markets, Zambia fell behind on her debts, becoming one of the most indebted countries on the planet relative to gross domestic product (GDP).

Despite putting Zambia at odds with her primary trading partners, Kaunda continued to support nationalist movements against minority-run white governments in Rhodesia (Zimbabwe), and other surrounding nations. Salaries stagnated and the price of mealie meal *(ground corn or maize)* kept rising.

These burdens continued to strain the Zambian economy until matters came to a head with the International Monetary Fund (IMF) in the late 1980's. Kaunda eventually lost the presidential election in 1991, and—unlike most other dictators—actually honored the vote.

39

Our last years in Zambia were the best. We lived with Dad and Mom and reveled in the lavish company of people from New Zealand, Denmark, America and Zambia. Friends became family. Uncles and Aunties didn't have to be blood relatives to fit the bill. All of Dad and Mom's friends were 'Uncle' and 'Auntie' to us. The appellation implied more intimacy than mister or missus without losing a respectful tone. I now have uncles and aunties on (almost) every continent.

Big family.

Correspondence school was made for Africa. We completed our course work in the morning and spent the afternoon with friends.

While we visited their houses frequently, our home became the meeting place of choice. Mom and Dad didn't mind having a house full of teenagers and welcomed them like they were their own children. They made themselves at home.

Most Sunday afternoons we hung out at Makoma Dam, to swim, suntan, cook boerewors and bread over the braai, and purchase cold sodas and biltong from the tuck shop. When I tired of swimming, mom challenged me to and beat me at Scrabble. (English and American spelling was allowed.)

Boerewors is a traditional Dutch sausage perfected by the Boers. Hence the name. Beef, lamb and pork blended with a mix of spices like toasted nutmeg, coriander, cloves and allspice created a fat-dripping, culinary masterpiece on the braai (or grill). Grilled boerewors on a piece of home-made bread toasted on the same grill could truly sate a man's wildest hunger.

Biltong is dried meat. To liken it to beef jerky is like comparing a fine Brie to Cheeze Whiz. A good piece of spicy biltong might keep a fellow busy for an hour.

Dad bought a sailboard and a couple of kayaks in South Africa, and we explored the Makoma Lake blissfully unconcerned about safety. Dad and Mom both windsurfed. (How did we win this 'lottery' to get such cool parents?) Julie and I learned the basics, and though I was too short for the boom (can you say powdered milk?), I managed well enough, I suppose. Mom was better at it.

Despite seeing a multitude of game in the wild, my aversion to the crocodile only came later.

The blue green waters of Lake Kashiba was another favorite haunt with family and friends. Pushing past Luanshya and turning east by Mpongwe, the road became increasingly nondescript.

The first time we went, Dad—mostly lost—drove down the dirt road. Road signs didn't happen often. Dad stopped to ask a villager for directions. The man shifted the axe on his shoulder and listened intently to Dad. Then he turned and pointed further down the road.

"You go and you go and you go, until you see some trees. Then you go until you see some more trees. It is just that side."

Dad thanked him and pulled away.

We were surrounded by trees.

We tootled off, trying to drive over the language barrier on a broken bridge. Dad figured the man was probably talking about specific and important trees.

Mango trees, for example, served a purpose similar to the mini marts and quick-stop convenience stores so prevalent in other countries. The woodsman's directions were loosely translated, *"Drive past the first convenience store. When you see the next one, stop and park. You'll have to walk from there.*"

Working on this assumption, Dad passed the first collection of mango trees and kept driving until he reached the next grove. We stopped and parked next to a ramshackle and abandoned mud block building that was being overtaken by bush, melting back into Africa. There was no direct road access to Lake Kashiba, so we parked and walked. Loaded up with coolers, lawn chairs and towels, we marched single file over the earthen footpath that snaked into the woods. A trumpeter hornbill's call overhead sounded so much like a baby crying it gave me the willies.

Legends and superstitions surrounded Lake Kashiba, whispers of evil, death and mass suicides. According to local legend, the lake was inhabited by a monster known as Isoka Ikulu who paralyzed men by grabbing their shadows and dragging them in.

The bush opened abruptly to reveal a lake, emerald clear and free of crocodiles. The cliff walls descended vertically into the lake as far as we could see, earning it the name, Sunken Lake. Cliff walls rose thirty feet above water level and extended straight down over five hundred feet. Fish that we reeled in from the depths suffered such a horrific case of the bends that their eyes popped out.

The cliff-banks started so suddenly it looked as if God had stuck his finger in the ground. It took several minutes to gear up for a dive off those rocks. I stood on the cliff, toes curled over the edge, staring down the long drop, counting 'ready, set, go' too many times for it to have any real meaning. When I did finally dive, the water smacked my head so hard it stung.

A massive tree hung over the water and provided the perfect place to attach a rope. Despite how others may imagine life in deep-dark-Africa, that was the only time I did the Tarzan-thing. And what fun it was! With a high grip on the rope I stepped into thin air, sailed down and away from the rocky face, legs gyrating, lungs screaming.

Letting go of a perfectly good rope is counter intuitive. Swinging back against the rock face is worse. Jumping from a rope swing creates (for just a few seconds) a feeling of complete weightlessness. At the apex of the swing, just after letting go, the earth seemed to lose its grip. Then gravity reached out, took hold and pulled hard. My body exploded into the crystal water in a spray of bubbles that started floating to the surface before I stopped going down. The further down I went, the colder the water became. The yawning emptiness opened beneath my feet. Finally, gravity lost to buoyancy, and my body stopped sinking. Beams of sunlight penetrated the water like spears, plunging into the deep before dissipating into the nothingness beneath. The whole lake was like a tube of water extending infinitely down, never narrowing, never reaching an end.

I swam toward the ceiling of air, pulling my way up the sunbeams, full of the thrill of sun, water, family and rope swings in the bush. We spent hours swinging, diving and exploring the crystal water.

No one charged admission. We didn't pay to park. We didn't have to rent a locker. There were no burn bans in place. There were no park attendants making sure we didn't fall off the rocks. In fact, there wasn't a single hand rail or safety feature of any kind. There were no mandatory recycling depositories. No warning signs or ridiculous rules.

No piped in music. No public restrooms. And usually, no one else was there.

Just our family and friends playing in wild, unspoiled Africa.

And life was good.

40

The wonder of sunshine and ample rainfall is that things grow. In fact, the longer the sun shines and the more it rains, the more nature tends to stretch out her long arms. Within this embrace, Zambia nurtures a fascinating collection of things that creep and crawl. These, of course, make for good stories. The inherent *danger* in mentioning these interesting critters alongside the requisite summary of snakes and spiders is that a reader may conclude Zambia is *all about* these creatures.

To do so is complete poppycock. A man can no more make an accurate determination of American life by watching the news or MTV. While they give a sort of *representation* of life in America, both are dead wrong. Neither cover the day-to-day wonder of neighborhood block parties, spaghetti dinners at the local fire hall, and hand-made ice cream. But we make these erroneous determinations all the time.

But the creepy crawlies of Africa *are* fascinating, so I'm going to write about them anyway.

A personal favorite is the putzi fly, or not so commonly known as the cordylobia anthropophaga. This little criminal lays her eggs in wet places, like laundry hanging on the wash line. The larvae hatch after a few days and, where available, will penetrate unbroken skin. The mere act of donning a clean pair of under-drawers gives this shameless creature access to regions unknown.

The larvae grows, making a hobbit-hole under the skin. As it grows, so does his abode, which develops into a painful furuncle (or boil). An African proverb states, 'Eating is better than being eaten.'

Okay. I made that up.

Most humans I have met take exception to non-rent-paying creatures taking up subcutaneous residence. The larval hobbit builds a door through which it can breathe and discharge it's fecal matter and whatever blood and puss happen as a byproduct of his development at your expense.

Evicting the putzi fly is nearly as exciting as television. A large maggot will have a large door. It is possible to see the creature poking his head out for a quick look around before burrowing back down.

Unmolested, the maggot will transition through three larval stages before leaving the host to pupate. To get it out before then, the creature must be lured to the opening and popped from his home. The best way to bring a putzi maggot to the surface is to smear a bit of Vaseline or petroleum jelly over the top of his breathe/waste hole and wait for him to come up for air. When he does, a deft squeeze at the sides should deliver the wiggling token which looks every bit like a miniature version of the Michelin Man.

In order to avoid this excitement, we practiced a skivvies-on-the-bottom routine, which is not what it sounds like. Fresh laundry went into the drawer at the bottom of the pile. Usually, by the time it came up to wear, the larvae had perished, thereby keeping one's nether regions uninhabited.

Mom also practiced the shake and fold technique. All laundry coming off the line was vigorously snapped, whip-like, before folding. This shook off the offending squatters, and as a result, fewer creatures took up residence in this shire. Both evasive maneuvers were considered more palatable than ironing *everything*.

The dogs, however, weren't so lucky. Lounging on a wet doormat resulted in a veritable collection of burrowing hitch-hikers.

At one time, I discovered an entire neighborhood of pustulating putzi portals on the side of our canine. Taking a fold of her elastic skin, I popped the first wrinkled and wiggling mass out onto the ground.

In a flash, the dog snapped it up, chewed and swallowed.

Sometimes karma is just plain gross.

Though not as prone to evoke a visceral quiver, the stick insect ranks near the top of his tribe in terms of sheer magic. That a blade of grass tumbling along in the wind might sometimes get up and walk stiffly off is very nearly like the talking trees of Narnia.

In terms of personality, however, it was hard to beat a praying mantis. Easy to handle, these creatures appeared to pay attention when addressed, cocking their head to the side, staring up into my face. They're the one insect that actually makes eye contact. A sign of intelligence? They made me laugh. A mantis might hang around for a while, walking placidly up and down my arm. Although they could fly, they rarely did and the mantis figured into a long line of temporary pets.

None among the insectivores were as lethal as the mosquito, but the tsetse fly garnered more hatred. I'm not sure how they were manufactured, but the little blighters were practically bullet proof. Their bite feels like hot acid. And while a good firm swat might send a tsetse fly to the dirt, he usually got up, brushed himself off and went on about his bloody business.

Dad warned me that the only sure way of shortening a tsetse fly's days was to follow the Biblical example of David with Goliath. Viz., strike off their heads. Unfortunately, the easiest way to catch a tsetse was to wait for one to bite. After smacking the offending creature, it fell, temporarily stunned. Dad showed me how to take the pernicious insect between his fingers and pick off its head.

Whereas Madame Guillotine might render her victims immediately immobile, a headless tsetse soldiered on for a while.

Ian Frew, fellow Sakeji-ite, monkey gang brother, bush dweller and friend, once kept a headless tsetse for an hour before the insect finally gave up and died.

Zambia waged a campaign against this fly because the trypanosomiasis—or sleeping sickness—it carried ruined domestic livestock in affected areas. Trypanosomiasis in cattle was first known by the Zulu word, nagana. Early explorer, doctor and missionary, David Livingstone, was the first to propose the possibility of a connection between nagana and the tsetse fly.

Although wild animals are trypanotolerant, the wasting disease results in a significant loss of condition in domestic cattle. Milk yields, fertility, and animal strength were all affected. As a result, tsetse fly ranges frequently coincided with regions suffering from malnourishment due to the lack of meat and dairy. Because cattle were not available for plowing and pulling, agricultural production also lagged behind.

The tsetse-borne parasites also affect people. In fact, the creature did its best to kill my dad when he was sixteen. Soaring fevers precipitated ice baths and a treatment of arsenic prescribed in doses considered high enough to kill the parasite and low enough—hopefully—not to kill him.

It worked, although Dad suffered extensive memory loss. Whether it was the result of fever or abuse at boarding school, we aren't entirely sure.

41

Ndola

Mama and Papa Lubwika (Zambian) served as surrogate grandparents. Their love extended beyond the irrelevancies of race, color and ethnicity. Mama Lubwika presided over my baptism when my blood grandparents were thousands of miles away.

No matter that the outdoor baptistry had only been filled to six inches on account of the water shortage. In a truly trans-ecumenical service, I was dunked, rolled, sprinkled and splashed before the pastor let me up.

There, among our Zambian family I drew my own line in the sand with, as the old song says, "no turning back." I was born in Africa because of other's passion for the extravagant love of Christ. But a man can't live off borrowed passion. My decision to get baptized was an outward sign that this love was my own.

It was only water, but it symbolized my decision to belong to God. A journey that began back at the goat-skinned drum.

We hung out with the church folk at Northrise, ECZ during the week. Sometimes on Sunday, I was conscripted to pass the offering basket.

And that was how this white-boy teenager stood staring awkwardly, while an amply-bosomed mama fished around in her blouse for a few **ngwee** (coins). They had made their escape from her fleshy purse.

Boobs were no big deal, teenager though I was. A culture of public breastfeeding inoculated me against such trivialities. Yet, I was keenly aware that boobs were taboo for white boys. The other white people in attendance might be offended at what they would consider my carnal-gawking. But the ngwee had most certainly escaped. I heard the coins tinkling around *way* underneath. Even the women beside her peered down her blouse and into the deep.

I seem to remember that Jesus told a similar story about a woman who lost a coin…

That was nothing. These coins were G.O.N.E.

At any rate, the big-mama probably wouldn't have minded if I had helped her get it out. But instead I made a study of the rafters while her neighbors offered advice.

I waited.

At last the wayward coins were retrieved from the valley lands, with much celebrating and a few chuckles.

42

Due to the fact that the world is (still) round, one can travel East or West out of Africa and (eventually) end up in the United States. Usually, we picked up intercontinental flights in Johannesburg, South Africa and made our way through Europe before ending up in the Pacific Northwest. On another occasion we flew East, making stops in Mauritius, Australia, New Zealand and Hawaii.

I have Uncles and Aunties everywhere. Mine is a strange family.

Because we lived in a place where grass huts were commonplace and the dollar carried weight, it didn't take much to feel fabulously wealthy. International travel accentuated the contrast.

Compared to most Americans, my parents made a pittance. Yet the nature of their work required significant travel, so by the time I was fourteen, I had almost as many countries stamped in my passports.

But Africa was my playground. Some people visit Africa once in their lifetime and marvel at the expansive savannas or subtropical woodlands replete with the big five: elephant, rhino, lion, cape buffalo and leopard. Their exotic destination was our home. Consequently, I grew up completely spoiled by the accessibility of wild places. Though the wild cats were elusive, crocodile, kudu, hartebeest, waterbuck, impala, hippo, elephant, and others were liberally splashed across the backdrop of my childhood.

We took family trips to the mysterious rock wall of ancient Great Zimbabwe and traveled further east where we clambered around the hilltop ruins of the magnificent Eastern Highlands. Because of the prevalence of biodegradable building materials, these are some of the few places where architectural evidence of Africa's deep history remains.

Lake Kariba was another favorite destination. The town of Kariba Heights started as a workers' camp on the hill overlooking Kariba Gorge where the Zambezi River once flowed uninterrupted on its way to the sea. The gorge proved to be the easiest place to bottle energy needed for cheap electricity—electricity needed to extract ore from the mines. Though the endeavor had the veneer of a development project, the quest to keep mining operations competitive drove its construction.

Kariba Heights morphed from a workers' camp into a tourist destination. Before war and political dysfunction worked their dark magic on Zimbabwe, the town drew masses to their all-inclusive resorts where local beer or Malawi Shandies accompanied a full, red sun sinking into the waters of Lake Kariba.

The resorts blossomed between villages. The folks who lived in Kariba Heights made an awkward peace with the elephants who ambled up tree-lined streets, stopping traffic and keeping tourists shop-bound as effectively as a tropical downpour.

Fishermen still plied their trade with nets from dugout canoes while more modern boats fished at night with lights to collect shimmering Tanganyika sardine, known locally as kapenta.

On one occasion we stayed at the Carribea Bay Resort. The Sardinian architecture blended with the occasional thatched pavilion to create a distinctly Mediterranean-African feel.

Cool stone walkways, broad tiles and shady niches inspired an early interest in architecture. Blue pools offered pristine swimming among an international clientele. The multiplicity of accents, colors and foods became a mainstay of my early life. I was no longer just a child of Zambia.

I was a child of the whole world.

Places like Carribea Bay functioned on an economic plateau markedly different from the nearby Zimbabwean villages. But that is the way it is the world over. Only occasionally are such disparate worlds situated so closely beside each other.

Living in a landlocked country like Zambia, the 2,100 square miles of the Kariba Reservoir offered a veritable ocean of water. Because crocodiles and hippos proliferated there, we limited swimming to resort pools or kayaked and windsurfed on the lake instead. One day I paddled beside Dad as he windsurfed out to Antelope Island. On the return, he rigged up a tow strap so I didn't have to paddle. I remember skimming along behind, watching the sun deepen the freckles on his shoulders, his eyes scan the open space, seeing the water draw away stress and fatigue. Water, I learned, was a tonic all its own. And Africa's beauty fed Dad's soul, as it did mine.

Only later did we learn that pilots flying over Kariba noticed crocodiles following the boats, hoping for an easy meal.

I suppose most other dads would hesitate to let their son make such a trek without a life vest in the company of Africa's wild creatures. But it was like that with Dad. He loved the bush. It was one of the ways Dad invited me into the adventure of living. He loved Africa's wild places. I think it was on our way back from Antelope Island when Dad brought Livingstone's words to mind. "If a man takes a drink from a river in Africa, he will always have to go back to quench his thirst."

African beauty isn't like the Himalayas or the Alps. Instead, she intoxicates with raw, untended, open places— the majesty of nature unencumbered.

Much like the path by the Victoria Falls with no rail to keep you in.

The Zambezi River thunders over the falls into Snake River Gorge, throwing up a veil of spray over visitors. The grassy edge above vanishes into a yawning open space any fool could walk over. The ground trembles—especially in rainy season, when the mile-wide cascade plummets three hundred and fifty feet into the gorge, frothing white with savage beauty. The column of spray obscures the canyon and is thrown back up into the sky. From miles away, it looks as if the river itself is on fire.

Dr. David Livingstone was primarily responsible for putting the upper regions of the Zambezi River on international maps. His early explorations into the dark hinterland resulted in his 'discovery' of the Mosi-ou-Tunya which he felt entitled to re-name the Victoria Falls. The 'Mosi-ou-Tunya,' which translates as 'Smoke which Thunders,' still pounds away at the rocky gorge just like it did then. Further downstream, the path of the Zambezi forever changed with the completion of the Kariba Dam in the late 1950's. Upstream, the Tonga lost their ancestral lands and were relocated to higher ground. Downstream, yearly inundations ceased and with it the annual, fertile deposits.

Africa captured Livingstone's affection. According to legend, he gave strict orders for his heart to be buried in Africa when he died.

The idea of his friends carving out Livingstone's heart doesn't evoke a pleasant picture, but they did and his heart is buried somewhere near the shores of Lake Bangweulu, in Zambia. His body is interred in England. How they managed to transport his dead body through the swelter of Africa all the way to England without pitching his festering remains unceremoniously into the sea is beyond my purview. But they did, and the Legend of Central Africa now rests alongside other great men and rascals in Westminster Abby.

I visited once. Names like Wilberforce, Darwin and Newton (as in Sir Isaac) keep Livingstone company. But the fact that he left his heart in Africa wasn't lost on me.

Something of my heart is still there as well.

43

1987

Seattle, Washington

We moved permanently to the States when I was thirteen. Whether I qualified as Zambian or African-American remained to be seen.

Leaving Africa began a few weeks before with teary farewells to friends we would probably never see again. We didn't know if we'd ever return. In the age before email and Skype brought distant people closer, it was like death without the finality.

Gone were the smells of bush fires and open air markets, frangipani blooms and boerewors on the grill. I left friends—the deep-wonderful-kind that shared a life-time of experiences. We left them milling around on the polished concrete floor of Ndola's airport terminal. I left a tiny town on the Copperbelt in a country few kids had ever heard about. That one awful day of leaving swallowed up my childhood. My whole world died.

Large, wet tears tumbled from Dad's eyes, too, running unmolested down his face. The oval plane window framed our last glimpses of home: rivers and streams crisscrossing green bush beyond the airport like the veins on the back of my hand.

Our journey to the States took us via points in Mauritius, Australia and New Zealand. We departed Auckland, New Zealand and touched down in Hawaii for a forty-five minute re-fuel. After eighteen hours on the plane we landed in California. A lifetime of airports blur and blend and share pieces with each other in my memory, but we finished our journey in Seattle.

The shiny aluminum tunnel of the airbridge into Seattle-Tacoma's International terminal muted the conversation of disembarking passengers. I followed lines of wrinkled pants down the too-clean blue carpet. Outside, the concourse hummed with jets queuing for departure. The excitement of travel and fun of seeing relatives I hadn't seen in four years, fought with overwhelming grief.

Leaving changed the channel of my life, and I ended up on a completely different program. I dressed wrong. Talked funny. Thought differently. But in America, I wasn't a minority, so no one noticed that in my heart I didn't belong.

I walked numbly from the airbridge to be greeted by a crowd of wonderful, too-hard hugs from waiting aunts, uncles, cousins, and grandparents. These were people I saw every four years or so. People who lived, at least from my perspective, on another planet entirely.

Americans.

Grandma wrapped me up in her perfect hug and said, "Welcome home."

She meant well. My loss was her gain. But Grandma didn't understand our trauma and her words dropped hot angry seeds into the soil of my pain. Like refugees, we packed up and left, not knowing if we'd ever see it again. I had just lost *everything* that was familiar. On the outside, I hugged and smiled. Inside, I was crying.

44

May 1987

We lived with Mom's parents in West Seattle for the summer. They had given up two children to Zambia. They missed out on watching five grandkids grow up. Now their oldest daughter (Mom) had come home.

They gave us the second floor of their house.

When I woke up, I strolled down to the kitchen to find one of Grandma's cinnamon rolls and a cup of coffee. Grandpa usually sat at the kitchen table, his sparsely-forested legs sticking out from underneath a tired terry-cloth bathrobe, sipping coffee and scowling at the daily crossword puzzle. He liked words, too.

Going to church in America was quite an event. Because most of Mom and Dad's sponsors came from these churches, we ended up being part of the required display when we visited. We hated it.

Sometimes Mom spoke to the youth. She got them involved. Julie and I helped. But how many times can a person teach a group of white faces a Zambian tribal greeting? The ordinary in Africa was now foreign and sensational, what with all that clapping and such.

Grandpa was a seasoned church-attender, but he understood that his grandkids didn't want to be on display, so he rescued us one Sunday from the circus act and the old ladies who pinched our cheeks and told us how they knew our mother when she was "only this tall."

He took us for doughnuts. Wonderful, maple-flavored pastries that made a mouth happy when paired with coffee.

Grandpa found time to take us to Alki Beach to fly kites. Only the kites got away, flying freely over the water, untethered and unencumbered.

And I daydreamed about doing the same. I had it all worked out. How to stow away on an airplane, travel back to Zambia, and. . . That's where the picture got fuzzy.

During the week, we started our day at Alki. Julie and Mom walked the beach. Dad and I ran. Then we finished with coffee from the Starbucks on Admiral Way. Mom and Dad believed in the resurrected Jesus, a personal God and good coffee.

We returned to Grandma and Grandpa's house where Julie and I worked on correspondence lessons. We knew we'd join the throng of public school students in a few short months, but I wasn't going to have the year's coursework done in time. The Afro-British school calendar didn't line up with the American one.

Julie and I gawked at distant fireworks celebrating America's Independence Day. I stared wide-eyed when the Blue Angels did a flyby trailing colored smoke. Eventually our plywood crates came— ferried overland by truck from Zambia to Durban or Cape Town where they were shipped to America and eventually delivered by truck to Grandma and Grandpa's house on the hill.

I unpacked my few special things. The snake skin of a Gaboon Viper from David Pedersen and the fangs which I kept in a glass vial with a rubber stopper. A giraffe tooth necklace from Aaron Salisbury. My knife collection. A preserved crocodile head. Various animal carvings. Dad's guitar. An international coin collection representing almost fifty countries. A chess set carved from malachite. A wire bicycle.

They littered the carpeted floor in a room that didn't smell like mine.

It brought a new level of finality, and I cried when I was alone.

After that summer, we moved into temporary housing in Portland and registered for public school.

45

Being a white middle school kid in Portland, Oregon sounds innocuous enough. But I felt like a foreigner in hiding. I guess eating elephant dramatically changes one's frame of reference.

Differences abounded. Even visiting a doctor was different. Zambia could boast, on average, one doctor for every 10,000 people. And because of Zambia's demographic distribution, these doctors were not widely accessible. Government clinics and hospitals often didn't have the most basic supplies.

In America, almost every person could boast having seen a family doctor, a specialist and a dentist within the course of a single year. Add to this the inordinately disproportionate availability of high quality medicines, technology, supplies, trained staff, logistical support and one begins to understand the disparity. People didn't stand in long lines all day waiting to be seen, nor get turned away because of lack of meds.

In Ndola, I joined cattle-chute style, vaccination lines of terrified boys. I watched the nurse plunge a mostly blunt needle into the boy's buttocks in front of me. She pulled the needle from the syringe and dropped it into the saucepan with a host of others being boiled. I saw her fish around for one she assumed to be 'clean enough' to pop on the end of the syringe before she repeated the procedure on D. Whitey. The point had gone flat, but she muscled it in with a grunt. Ow! (This in the soon to be discovered hotbed of AIDS.)

Not in America. Here, *everything* medical came sharp, individually wrapped for single use and was subsequently discarded. The salvaged medical waste of a single day might have sustained the entire nation of Zambia for a year. The doctors' offices smelled clean with none of the African body smell.

America had fast food chains. Grocery stores had *everything*. Seven kinds of peanut butter. Two hundred cereals. Eight varieties of maple syrup. More peanut butter. Twenty varieties of *already-sliced* bread. Real butter. Yogurt. Fresh veggies and frozen veggies and sea food and deli items and flashy signs and fully stocked shelves. And the floors in the grocery store had no tiles missing.

Electricity, water and trash collection were taken for granted. Americans lived in a world where mass transit systems worked *all the time*. One may even take a picture of a bridge without the camera being confiscated by the military. Police showed up in real time. Emergency services were available. Mail and delivery systems happened like clockwork. Packages didn't have to be opened at the post office where the post master checked for items to tax or take for himself.

There were cars, cars, cars, all driving on the wrong side of the road. One tried to kill me because I looked right instead of left before I crossed the street.

Though I spoke English, it didn't always help me.

Mom and Dad got us ready for school. *Remember*, said they, "This is an eraser, *not* a rubber."

And Julie practiced, "This is an eraser *not* a rubber. This is an eraser, *not* a rubber."

It would never do to raise one's hand and ask for a rubber in class.

In America, fries and chips were different foods. Torches were flashlights. A car had a hood and trunk instead of a boot and bonnet. My spelling suffered setbacks. 'Neighbor' not 'neighbour.' 'Labor' not 'labour.'

171

Even the date was backward. Instead of *day/month/year* it was *month/day/year*.

Girls were hitting on me and I didn't know what they were talking about. Mom chose to translate or not, depending.

Lord, have mercy!

Julie was the only one who understood my world. But she was in high school and I was suffering through the throes of middle school in a completely different part of town.

The coach saw her swim in gym class and asked if she wanted to join the water polo team.

She asked if it involved swimming.

She didn't know she scored a starting position on the varsity team. They might have told her, but she didn't know what it meant to have a *starting position* and didn't have a clue what *varsity* meant.

I knew about kayaking and enjoyed watching rugby. To most of my peers, rugby was an erudite sport played by a few ivy league schools who wanted to pretend America still belonged to the British Empire. While kids in America were going to soccer practice, I was playing squash. No one at my new school had ever heard of squash.

Kids my age had grown up going out for pizza and playing Pac Man. My American peers knew about football, television, music and celebrities. And they talked about them *all* the time.

It was as if these things *really mattered*. Even clothing was important to almost everyone and *I didn't even notice*. I could have worn the same outfit every day and never given it a second thought. No one told me that plaid and prints weren't friends. My idea of a matching outfit was pants *and* a shirt. If I was covered, it matched.

46

We didn't have a television our first year in the U.S. The world of American media swarmed out of reach. I had no appetite for radio, and the most basic file of sport's terminology was missing from my cabinet.

Though I grew up *owning* a basketball, I knew nothing of the rules and vocabulary associated with the game.

I tried basketball. Actually, I followed my recently returned, South African-American cousin, Matthew, into it. He was entirely athletic and bursting early into manhood. I was not. I understood the point of basketball, however. The good guys (your team) put the ball in that ring over there. The bad guys put it in the hoop on the other side. The equation was simple. Ball + Basket = Good.

I stepped onto the court and the coach called out something about a 'pick' and 'traveling.' Tooth picks, ice picks, or picks for digging in hard soil?

I understood the words. I felt the coach's frustration: What kind of a kid goes out for basketball and doesn't know about traveling?

I certainly knew about travel. I'd been to the beaches of Mauritius and Australia, seen the sulfur springs of New Zealand, visited Sidney Opera House, and got sunburn in Hawaii. I'd taken a drink from the source of the Zambezi River, and stood in its spray at the Victoria Falls. I'd seen the waves kiss the beaches of Lake Malawi, caught my first tiger fish in Lake Tanganyika, walked the streets of London, visited black townships in South Africa and knew about 'apartheid.'

I'd eaten elephant, hippo, and various village foods I didn't recognize.

I had traveled halfway around the world four times. I knew about travel.

The bench on the sidelines had been varnished several times but was peeling and chipped. Not a place to get comfortable.

Could no one see this raging *differentness* I felt?

I was well on my way to becoming a perfectly maladjusted young man. Mom noticed my retreat into a shell, never speaking, never interacting. I didn't *want* to learn how to be an American. In my opinion, Americans filled their time with the irrelevant. What difference did it make what I wore to school?

Why should I care what sports team was playing or who was the hottest, latest movie star? What did it matter if some musician broke up with his girlfriend? There was, I reasoned, a whole world of wonderful, desperate, suffering people out there.

And Americans didn't have a clue. Or didn't care. I couldn't tell which.

So I turned to judgement. I railed against America's preoccupation with media and sports and fashion and popularity. I derided the relentless pursuit of wealth and success. And condemnation became my self-defense against feeling completely out-of-my-world. I was an alien with no desire to fit in.

47

Middle school, I decided, is a trial run for hell. There, I retreated and interacted almost exclusively with two people: a Korean kid whose parents had recently immigrated to the U.S. and my South African cousin, Matt. Matt and Lisa had moved to the States just the year before to finish up their schooling.

Our parents tried to prepare us for things like rubbers and combination locks. But they had lived so long overseas they weren't getting it right either. In America, the first number in the combination is always to the *right*. Right, left, right. *Not* left, right, left. No wonder we couldn't get the damn thing open and the principal had to get involved. Just having the right numbers doesn't work.

In order to help me adjust, I was invited to collect money from students buying hot lunches in the school cafeteria. I needed to learn the mystery of American coinage. The one, five and ten cent pieces had an identity crisis. Why one cent should be *larger* than ten cents was beyond me.

Then I had to learn their names. Nickel. Dime. Penny. Familiar words to everyone except me.

I couldn't believe how much food was discarded! Kids sometimes threw away half their lunch, while I was busy finishing everything in my paper bag. I was genuinely aghast. After all, there were children in Africa who needed that to live. I'd met some of them. But though American's ate mostly for pleasure, even they needed food to stay alive; they just forgot that part most of the time.

175

Eighth grade locker rooms hold a particular horror for the uninitiated. They embody the no-mans-land between moral establishment and the hormonal chaos of almost-men. Our gym teacher had enough good sense to avoid the locker room except for shouting an occasional 'hurry up' that echoed off tile floors.

I clutched a paper lunch bag stuffed with clean gym clothes, trying desperately to look comfortable on this other planet. No one told me lunch bags just *weren't cool* to carry gym clothes. Most of the time I maintained absolute silence. Some thought I didn't know how to speak English. When I did, many struggled to understand my bizarre accent.

Keeping safely silent in the throng of boys, I pulled out my school shorts and matching tee.

My hands froze.

Buried between folds I spotted a fringe of lace. I was uninitiated, but I wasn't stupid. Boys wouldn't care that Mom inadvertently folded my sister's underpants with my clothes. And they certainly wouldn't believe me. I knew that moving forward was to invite direct assault.

In my naiveté, I didn't know that in certain circles, such a scenario could make me look like a conquering hero.

Options?

Get sick—suddenly and violently.

I could feign paranoia, run screaming from an imaginary demon.

I could pull the fire alarm or pretend to have lost my gym clothes.

The last would be difficult, considering they were in my hands.

In the end, I did the only thing I knew how to do. Tell the truth.

I made a plan: Laugh it off. Making light of what I didn't understand had become a coping strategy and dysfunctional way of filling in the '*other*' bubble in the race category.

Pinching a pink seam, I pulled the offending garment from its place, dangling the irreverent lingerie in front of me.

In a matter of seconds, the lace drew the attention of every man-boy in the locker room. Hooting and laughter erupted. Everyone had an opinion as to how a girl's panties got with my gym clothes.

For those eternal minutes, I may have been the only red African-American on the planet.

48

Outside school, a youth pastor named Tony Pollard was brave enough to reach past the thorn trees I'd established around myself. I spent hours with Tony and Michael Wooten, another white-boy missionary kid displaced from Portugal. Tony and Mike were friends I didn't deserve. They pulled me into life, in spite of myself. Together they put flesh on America.

Tony took us hiking around the woods of the Multnomah Falls, snow camping on Mount Hood and backpacking on the Sisters Mountains.

As snow never visited Zambia, I knew nothing about camping in it. But Tony and his mountaineering friend Scott took us anyway. We climbed the middle sister and camped above a cliff. We hiked up to the saddle and slid down into the cloud cover on trash bag sleds.

Back at camp, Tony warmed up spaghetti his wife had sent along and made hot chocolate over a hissing stove.

In the morning, the sun came up, pinking the clouds beneath us and blushing the faces of Mount Jefferson and Mount Washington in the distance.

Where I thought America was self-absorbed, frivolous and insincere, Tony showed me that America was beautiful.

And while I thought it betrayed my Zambian patriotism, Mike reminded me it was okay to love it.

But I wasn't ready. So I remembered Zambia out loud. All the time.

God bless them for putting up with me.

49

The great disorientation of my life had been not knowing where I *wanted* to fit in. I understood that the process of becoming an American was as simple as saying 'yes.' Because I already had a U.S. passport, I didn't have to sit for citizenship exams. It might have done me good. There's something powerful about engaging the will.

But when the internal parking brake is pulled, not much progress will be made.

My first year back in the States, I not only had the parking brake on, I made sure the wheels were blocked and the tires slashed. I decided, in no uncertain terms, that I was NOT going to become an American.

Living the parallel reality in Zambia was easier. Easier, perhaps, because I was already white enough that people expected me to be different. D. Whitey. No explanation necessary.

In the States, I had a 'funny' accent, but looked like most everyone else. Early on I determined not to open any relational doors that were not absolutely necessary. According to my parents, we returned to the States so I could get an education.

So I became a student.

Mom grew concerned when I started making all 'A's.' Something was definitely wrong with this boy.

I didn't speak to anyone. I was so quiet that cheerleader Kim, a few lockers down, wondered aloud that I might not speak English. When she heard I was from Africa, she asked, "Did you wear a loin cloth and live in a grass hut?"

Welcome to Middle School America.

I stared back and mumbled, "No."

But her ethnocentrism was no more profound than Zambians who 'understand' the American culture as being as violent or sexually permissive as reflected by American media. (A sobering thought.)

The buzz of America swirled around the backdrop of my life in Africa. This wasn't a parallel world.

This. Was. Another. Planet.

The bone-jarring contrasts of relative opulence chaffing against the backdrop of how most of 'my' Africa lived, put me in a downward spiral. I went from being the richest kid in town to one of the poorest, though it took me five years to notice.

I reverted to a judgementalism that railed against everything I saw. The internal grind robbed me of sleep, barricaded relationships and worked like a toxin.

The rotting cheese in my mind turned blue and started to get hairy.

50

We moved from our temporary housing in Portland after just a few months. To stay in the same school district, Mom and Dad rented a three-bedroom apartment off Powell Boulevard. The woman in the apartment below thumped her broom handle on the ceiling if we were too loud. A paved parking lot took up what space remained, and a tiny balcony looked out over a fenced-in scrubby field beyond.

I was a long way from the wilds of Africa.

Resentment chafed. My world of experience didn't fit. People didn't understand me, nor I, them. I rarely gave them a chance.

Then we got the report. Dad took the phone call from a friend in Canada. I don't know how word traveled, but Dad gathered us around and cried through the news:

Ian Frew was dead.

Ian, who was always smiling. We climbed trees and ate wild fruit together. We lived together at Chizela, my first home, and then Sakeji. His older brother was my big brother during the first harrowing term at boarding school. We visited them before leaving Africa. He showed us the uni-cycle he rode in a rural parade and laughed that they introduced him as "Ian Flew on his Unique Cycle."

On his last term break, Ian and Uncle Keith (his dad) took a rafting trip down the Kabompo River with a few other men. Men I knew. Uncle Ken. Uncle Gordie. Not blood relatives, but uncles just the same.

Their raft capsized and Ian did his part to collect gear from the water. His feet were tough and he ran through the elephant grass growing thick along the bank to grab what he could from the river and drag it ashore. Then he dived in to join the men on the opposite side.

At that moment, Uncle Gordie saw a nearby swirl of water and yelled for Ian to get out of the river.

Ian retreated back the way he'd come. He was in only two feet of water when the crocodile took him.

His father and Uncle Gordie watched the creature pull him under. Impossibly, Ian managed to break free, surface, and scream for help.

But the croc took him again, and he disappeared forever.

Without shoes, the weeping men walked barefoot, carrying the unbearable home.

Ian's three older siblings were in Canadian universities at the time.

We grieved the loss and the horror of it. Yet another out-of-this-world marker in my world of experience no one would understand.

Or so I thought.

The truth is that plenty of people have lost someone. Death, in any form, is a hideous aberration of life. People get that. People understand and might have related to me in that. People didn't need to know Africa for me to relate to them.

There is our humanity. Our desire for belonging. The practice of sharing a smile or a meal can still bridge gaps created by worlds at odds.

51

1988

I guess we didn't want to get static, so a year after moving to the Pacific Northwest, Dad received an invitation to work as Dean of Men and sometimes-professor at Lancaster Bible College. It meant relocating 2,800 miles to Lancaster County, Pennsylvania.

We huddled over the contract and all held the pen as Dad signed his name. He was agreeing to take a job, I was agreeing to engage my will in the process of starting over. Again.

Mom and Dad left early and drove across the country with a rental truck. Julie and I followed later, flying in to Philadelphia.

They picked us up from the airport. I stared out the car window as we quit the airport and threaded our way out of the concrete snarl of Philadelphia. The city fell away behind as we drove west toward Lancaster.

The rented farm house hadn't been renovated in quite a while, but it was spacious. After the apartment in Portland, it felt palatial. Here, at last, was space to breathe. Expansive corn fields surrounded the property. Aside from the family who lived in the other half of the house, we had no immediate neighbors. An Amish family lived down the road and for a while, the sound of horse and buggy brought me to the window.

Freight trains lumbered slowly over a rail line that cut through corn fields across the road. In front of it, a crypt held bodies of farmers who settled the area in the 1800's. People who lived and died on this land. The stone face of the crypt testified to the world that they chose to live there.

I wondered what that might be like.

Though it persisted in my daydreams, Zambia seemed farther away in Lancaster County. Distant. More inaccessible.

The surrounding farm lanes and country roads drew me to walk and think and talk to God. I sat behind the barn to watch the sunset. Soon August clouds thrust up against the heavens were robed in purples and pinks. Lightning bugs rose from the fields like sparks from a fire. Cicadas called from oak trees, singing their circular songs into humid summer nights.

This was the breadbasket of Pennsylvania with Amish families who drove real buggies and plowed their fields with teams of mules. It carried the deep history of men and women who had come here to start a new life. Every single one had left somewhere else to settle here. Lancaster County was more than covered wooden bridges, underground railroads, historic houses and cemeteries dating back to the Civil War.

It was a place for me to get over myself and start again. I decided, then, to *be* where I was.

Epilogue

Everyone looks at the world through a key-hole. In one way or another, our keyholes determine how we view ourselves. People all look for a way to define themselves and others. Everyone wants to know where they're from, who they are.

Am I an African-born American or an African-American or a foreign-born American or a nothing?

It matters deeply.

But passports and birth certificates don't provide accurate labels.

Certainly—the world over—people are looking for an anchor point. A place they can come home to and feel safe. A place where they can get on with the business of work, family and faith without fear of being raped in their fields, or molested by government officials.

While culture, experience and story make us who we are, these don't guarantee belonging. The poem posted on the placard beneath the Statue of Liberty calls out to this yearning, and in her invitation is the hint of a promise. Only one problem: America still *has* the tired, poor, tempest tossed, and homeless, huddled masses.

In the failure of Liberty's promise I discovered *a place cannot offer belonging*. It isn't found in birthright, birth certificate, linguistic or religious heritage.

Once, I asked God why boarding school had to be part of my story. He said, 'to taste the orphan heart.'

Not exactly the answer I was looking for. But hurt birthed an inner quest to find something *real* to fill the void. I tried places. I tried people. I tried occupations.

None of them worked, and my orphan heart wasn't satisfied.

Jesus told a story about a wayward, expatriate son. The son took his share of the family money and set out to another country determined to fill his void. But a famine conspired against him and his friends dried up when the money ran out.

He hit bottom. Lost. Broken. And hungry.

Disillusioned, the young man headed back to his father's house and found what he'd been looking for all along.

His father was waiting for him, saw him coming and ran out to meet him.

He didn't ask where the young man had been. He didn't draw up a payment schedule for the money his son had wasted. He didn't ask for a passport. Instead, he offered himself.

The unconditional embrace.

I, too, have found that Divine embrace. It is for those with the wrong passport, no place, no home, no sense of belonging. It is for the empty and the hungry, the hurting and broken. It is for immigrants and orphans, lawyers and losers.

It has become my anchor point.

And that, to borrow a line from Robert Frost, has made all the difference.

Glossary

BaKaonde: Kaonde people, a tribal group traditionally residing in Zambia's Northwestern Province and the Democratic Republic of Congo. kiKaonde is understood by 350,000 people.

biseke: Zambian full-kernel maize beer

braai: charcoal or malasha grill

grass slasher: A wooden handle attached to a 40" blade designed to cut dense grass and weeds; in Zambia the slasher was used as an alternative to a lawn mower.

Chizela: Bush Bible School established in 1948 among the BaKaonde people

kiKaonde: the language of the BaKaonde

kisapi: traditional patterned cloth worn by women, usually wrapped around the waist; also used to carry infants on the back

Kwacha: Zambian paper money; translated it means, '*it dawns*'

lekker: an Afrikaans word meaning 'cool'

loo: bathroom

lorry: truck

malasha: with the absence of industrially produced charcoal, enterprising villagers sold malasha—a substitute. Wood was stacked in racks and then covered with a thick layer of sod. The piles burned slowly for many days. Once the pile was uncovered, the sod was removed and the resulting product broken into manageable chunks and packed in empty mealie meal bags. The malasha usually so over filled the bag, that it looked like a black and dirty ice cream cone. The protruding layer of malasha was lashed into place with bark rope. It was then wheeled on the ubiquitous black bicycle into town for sale. (At that time, every Zambian bike was black.)

malekeni: bicycle tire rubber, salvaged to use as bungee cord-like tie-down, etc.

mpazhi: army ants

Mukinge: Bush Mission Hospital, founded in 1952

Ngwee: Zambian coinage; translated it means, '*bright*'

Piccanins: term used for all young children, not derogatory as commonly used in America.

rice cakes: Not to be confused with the pressed cardboard-like disks purveyed by American grocers, the rice cake is the pièce de résistance. Boiled rice was shaped into patties or balls and fried. A perfect rice cake had a crisp brown exterior and a warm soft belly.

Sakeji: Brethren British Boarding School initially established for children of missionaries in Zambia.

Also by Dwight Kopp

THE ZAMBEZI CHRONICLES

The Contract*

Critical Fault*

Cover of Darkness

THE MODERATOR SERIES

The Moderator

The Coma

Grid Lock

*Available in audio from audible.com and iTunes.com

On Facebook at www.facebook.com/dwightkoppbooks

On the web at www.dwightkopp.com

Acknowledgments

Writing about one's childhood is a complicated thing. Fiction is easier, for the author does what we all wish to do with our own life: make the pieces fit together. The truth of a life is messier, more complicated.

Reading through a life from someone else's perspective isn't easy either, so I want to thank my parents Tim and Carol, and sister, Julie, who laughed and cried and cried and laughed as they proof-read my drafts, helping to jog my memory and to keep me from telling lies.

My thanks as well to Doe, my wife, who read and edited the manuscript almost as many times as I did. Martha and Jay Squaresky, once again, were invaluable early readers, just as they were with my first six novels. Thanks.

Of course, any remaining errors are my own fault.

CPSIA information can be obtained
at www.ICGtesting.com
Printed in the USA
LVOW13s2304080817
544321LV00009B/184/P